Vocabulary Development Using Roots and Riddles

by Claudia Vurnakes
illustrated by Tony Waters

FS-10204 Vocabulary Development Using Roots and Riddles
All rights reserved—Printed in the U.S.A.
Copyright © 1996 Frank Schaffer Publications, Inc.
23740 Hawthorne Blvd.
Torrance, CA 90505

TO THE TEACHER

Take a double-barreled approach to vocabulary development! This resource book for your middle school and high school students features common Latin and Greek roots. Alongside traditional dictionary study activities, you will find wacky vocabulary-based riddles and mind-stretching usage activities. The purposes of this book are to encourage students to "play around" with words, to help students discover the fun words can provide, and to enable students to experience the power of words. In order to challenge students with various learning styles, each four-page unit in this book presents the unit vocabulary words in four different ways.

- **Teacher Resource** pages provide introductory background and suggest creative plans for small group interaction and independent thinking. Your students will fly paper "missiles" when they study the -Miss- / -Mitt- root, pantomime a primate reading a primer when they work with the -Primo- root, and locate world ports on a map as they learn words that share the -Port- root.

- **Reading for Meaning** makes it possible for students to experience the unit words in context, with a brief story about Rootster, a globe-trotting pilot who searches for exciting words. In addition to the featured vocabulary, your class will pick up tidbits of information about architecture, Mardi Gras, temples, and other topics as they travel with Rootster.

- On **Rootster's Riddles** pages, students solve puzzling questions using their knowledge of the unit vocabulary. Knowing that the -Ped-/-Pod- root indicates a connection with the foot, your class will chuckle (or groan!) when they read, *What is a podiatrist's favorite mushroom?* and find that the answer is *A footstool.*

- **Working With Words** provides opportunities for students to use the new words and apply what they have learned. Once they have studied the words and their definitions, the students are challenged to put the words to work. These activities may include correcting usage errors, re-writing wordy sentences, and filling in the blanks in thought-provoking passages.

With some common roots spawning more than a hundred modern derivatives, knowledge of these basic building blocks provides students with a powerful tool for vocabulary development. Make your students' introduction to the world of vocabulary an exciting one. Use the activities in this book to help them discover that words will never fail them—for interest, for amusement, for clarity of thought, and for expanding horizons.

-VOC- to call, to speak, voice

advocate	*vocal*
avocation	*vocalist*
invocation	*vocation*
provoke	*vociferous*
revoke	*voucher*
vocabulary	*vowel*

Unit Kickoff

Introduce the -VOC- unit with a student pantomime of the words *provoke*, *revoke*, and *invoke*. Prepare ahead of time cards describing appropriate actions—one student teasing another for the word *provoke,* a person praying for *invoke,* and a police officer confiscating a driver's license for *revoke.* Write the the three words on the chalkboard. As students act out the situations, have the class match the words to the situations. Discuss the idea common to all three words, the root meaning of -VOC- (to call).

Word Exploration Ideas

Offer this familiar old adage as a good example of the word *vociferous*: "The squeaky wheel gets the oil." Lead students in developing other sayings (such as "The screaming baby gets the first bottle.") that convey the concept of loudness.

Invite students and staff to share unusual *avocations* with your class.

Hold a discussion about rules or laws that the students think should be revoked. Then have each student write a persuasive letter to express his or her views.

In a discussion of *advocate*, point out that the word implies a type of relationship. Every advocate speaks on behalf of someone else. Ask students to suggest individuals and groups that need the support of an advocate. Then select one and, as a class, write a Help Wanted ad for a qualified advocate. Make it a humorous ad if you wish. (Example—Help Wanted: Aardvark Advocate. Experienced individual needed to speak out on behalf of misunderstood African mammal. Must be able to travel to zoos across the country. Benefits include generous meals of ants and termites.)

Conduct a classroom or schoolwide survey to determine the students' favorite *vocalists*. For some fun, play short segments of current hits and ask students to "Name That Vocalist."

READING FOR MEANING
-VOC-
to call, to speak, voice

> Greetings and welcome aboard! I'll say it again, a little louder this time: GREETINGS AND WELCOME ABOARD!

This is your **vociferous** pilot speaking, Roger Rootster. Please check your flight **vouchers** carefully. Stowaways tend to **provoke** me. We have an exciting ride ahead, with destinations mysterious and unknown. Flying is my **vocation**, but words are my true passion, my **avocation**. I am a **vocalist** of **vowels**, an **advocate** of verbs, a juggler of adjectives, a wizard of words. I am **vocal** about **vocabulary** and serious with synonyms. I believe language should be fun, and I get very **provoked** when people make it boring.

So come on! Buckle your seat belts! Once we begin, there will be no turning back, no **revoking** of our terrific travel plans. Say your **invocations** now, and get ready for real adventure in the exciting world of words.

ROOTING FOR MEANING
-VOC-

Write definitions for the boldfaced words. Refer to a dictionary. Include a root meaning (call, speak, or voice) in each definition.
Example: evoke—to call back

ROOTSTER'S -VOC- RIDDLES

Read the vocabulary riddles below. Write the letter of the matching answer in each blank.

_____ 1. What do you call a person who loves to make avocational use of yarn?

_____ 2. What did the canary say when it swallowed the student's vocabulary list?

_____ 3. What do good little wolfmen learn in Monster Kindergarten?

_____ 4. What do you call an advocate for short people?

_____ 5. What kind of vocation did the Absent-Minded Professor find?

_____ 6. What did the Absent-Minded Professor name his new invention for removing cholesterol from eggs?

_____ 7. What is the name of the vociferous singing group that comes from the state south of New York?

_____ 8. How did Show-off Shawn describe his method of dealing with teachers?

_____ 9. What's another name for the Dieter's Invocation?

_____ 10. A pizza maker loved to vocalize whenever he tossed the dough. He was so good, his friends urged him to enter a talent contest. What did the pizza maker call his act?

_____ 11. A man made the *Guinness Book of World Records* for his extraordinary vocal abilities. What did the bumper sticker on his car say?

_____ 12. All the city subways were named after colors: Red, Orange, Green. The Purple train had just left the station when the conductor noticed a vampire chasing it down the track, fangs bared and eyes glowing. What did the vampire say when the frightened conductor finally opened the door?

a. Revoke-A-Yolk

b. Pray-and-Weigh

c. "Wordy bird! Wordy bird!"

d. Their vowels and howls

e. A knit nut

f. "I v-v-vorgot my v-v-violet v-voucher!"

g. "Singing and Flinging"

h. A thingamabob job using his whatchamadoodle noodle

i. A Shorter Supporter

j. "Provoke'em and joke'em!"

k. Loud And Proud Of It!

l. The Noisy Boysies From Joisey

WORKING WITH
-VOC-
WORDS

It is Music Awards Night, and Rootster is doing the honors! For each award category below, find the matching song title or lyric.

1. Best Invocation: _____
2. Best Use of Vocabulary: _____
3. Best Musical Advocate for Animals: _____
4. Best Vocational Song: _____
5. Most Vociferous Music Video: _____
6. Best Avocational Song: _____
7. Best Non-Vocal Music Video: _____
8. Most Provoking Lyrics: _____
9. Most Unusual Vocalists: _____
10. Best Use of Vowels: _____
11. Most Creative Use of Vouchers: _____
12. Best Song for Revoking a Dog Tag: _____

a. "Anthem for Angry Voices"

b. "Hand It Over, Rover"

c. "Prayer for the Children"

d. "I've been working on the railroad, all the livelong day…"

e. "The Silence of the Stars"

f. "Take home a stray, Feed it today!"

g. "Buy a ticket on the Love Train, Life will never ever be the same. . ."

h. "Sing it out loud, I'm smart and I'm proud…"

i. "Winning Her Heart with Great Words"

j. "You and I don't make a connection, Think I'll start a stamp collection. . ."

k. "A-la-la-la-la, oo-oo-oo-ah! u-ee-u-ee-u ee, oo-oo-oo-ah!"

l. "Song Sung by a Dozen Chickens"

-BENE-, -BON- good, well

benediction	benison	bonny
beneficial	bona fide	bonus
benevolent	bonbon	bon voyage
benign	bon mot	bounteous
		bounty

Unit Kickoff

Read a few **bonny** folk poems by Robert Burns to your class. Students who have never been exposed to the Scots' dialect will enjoy hearing such selections as "A Red, Red Rose," "To a Mountain Daisy," "To a Mouse," "Auld Lang Syne," and others. Point out that the vocabulary words in this unit have come from ancient Rome and France, as well as Scotland. The English language is a true melting pot, enriched by many cultures.

Word Exploration Ideas

On the American frontier, **bounty** hunters found plenty of work tracking down wanted criminals and dangerous beasts. Assign students the task of creating Old West posters that promise a generous bounty for the capture and return of a fictitious desperado.

Have your students write **benedictions** about the end of a month, season, or year.

Be armchair travelers and plan a trip to a dream destination. Create travel brochures, discuss what to pack, and plan a **bon voyage** party.

Discuss the implications of the political term **benevolent** dictator. Is this type of leader good for a country? What conditions might lead to this situation? Should a parent be the benevolent dictator of his or her family?

In today's fast-food culture, many students do not realize that **bonbons** can be prepared at home. Bring in a hot plate (or use your home economics lab) to prepare a simple boiled sugar candy recipe such as toffee, divinity, or lollipops. Have your students write creative descriptions or advertisements of the bonbons.

Post the heading *Guide to the **Bona Fide*** on your bulletin board and send students out to collect trademarks, logos, and other common marks of authenticity. Discuss the ways copycat companies imitate bona fide bestsellers.

READING FOR MEANING
-BENE-, -BON-
good, well

Why is the airplane full of balloons, Rootster?

How else do we throw ourselves a **bon voyage** party? Come on, everyone! Throw balloons, throw **bonbons**, throw **benevolent bons mots**, too. And while you're at it, throw some of that **bounteous** baggage out the window! Only **bona fide** essentials are allowed on this trip—a notebook, a pencil, and eyes ready to see the rich **bounty** of Vocab land. Are you folks ready?

We passengers give the eager young pilot **benisons** and **benedictions**. The Captain of Cool points the plane into the **benign** clouds. We settle down for the flight, many of us snatching a **beneficial** snooze. Soon, a **bonny** world unfolds beneath us.

"It won't be long now!" chuckles Rootster. "But before we land, I have a special **bonus** for you. Lunch courtesy of Chef Rootster!"

ROOTING FOR MEANING
-BENE-, -BON-

Write definitions for the boldfaced words. Include the root meaning (good or well) in each definition.

Example: bonus—something good given in addition to what is required

ROOTSTER'S -BENE-, -BON- RIDDLES

Match the clues on the left with the correct rhyming answers on the right.

_____1. A bumper crop of Canadian police on horseback.

_____2. A prayer said over a dinner of deer meat.

_____3. The best kind of woman to marry

_____4. A harmless complaint

_____5. An "A" on a report card

a. A bona fide bride

b. A beneficial initial

c. Mounty bounty

d. Venison benison

e. A benign whine

Match each group or animal to the appropriate sign listed below.

_____ 6. Brand-new ministers and priests
_____ 7. Professional cherry pickers who want to make pie
_____ 8. People with friends leaving on a long trip
_____ 9. A group of dieting adults
_____10. Pirates in need of a beauty makeover
_____11. An old maids' social club
_____12. Society of Comedians
_____13. A dog hungry for a nice juicy bone

f. Bounteous Bachelors Ahead

g. Bonus Berries for Overtime

h. Bons Mots for Sale or Trade

i. All Bonbons Banned

j. For Sale: Big Book of Benedictions

k. The Bonny Buccaneer Salon

l. Bon Voyage Supplies Here

m. Open: Benevolent Butcher

WORKING WITH -BENE-, -BON- WORDS

benediction	*benison*	*bonny*
beneficial	*bona fide*	*bonus*
benevolent	*bonbon*	*bon voyage*
benign	*bon mot*	*bounteous*
		bounty

Rootster's motto is K.I.S.S.—Keep It Simple, Silly! Can you rewrite each wordy sentence below in six words or less?

1. The religious leader pronounces the blessing at the end of the worship service.

2. "Have a safe trip! Don't forget to mail me written communications," she called.

3. He was able to stay alive because of the good yield that he harvested from his garden.

4. The gourmet cook employed by the restaurant spooned out marshmallow nougat and then covered it with chocolate. It tasted terrific!

5. The man put down a large deposit and gave his word that he would purchase the house.

6. Although the oozing sore on the man's leg looked repulsive, it was not harmful to his health in the least.

7. Every juvenile individual should experience the kindly giving nature of his mother's mother.

8. The individual employed to perform a job received an extra payment for going above and beyond the call of duty.

9. She was a young lady blessed with a highly attractive external appearance.

10. Repeat words of gratitude to the almighty power of the universe prior to partaking of your daily bread.

11. A quick, clever remark may be fun to make, but it sometimes hurts another's feelings.

12. The single best way to enhance one's time spent doing schoolwork is to ensure that the immediate environment is peaceful and quiet.

-MIN- small, less

menu	*minority*
mince	*minstrel*
miniature	*minuet*
minimum	*minuscule*
minister	*minute*
minor	*minuteman*

Unit Kickoff

Create interest for the -MIN- unit words with a musical interlude. Play recordings of one or more of Beethoven's minuets and Stephen Foster's show tunes. Explain that these two different styles of music share the root word -MIN-. Beethoven wrote music for an extremely popular dance of his day, the *minuet*, while Foster wrote in the tradition of the traveling entertainer, the *minstrel*. Send students to a dictionary to discover how the root meaning for -MIN- (small or less) applies to both terms. A *minuet* is a dance; a *minstrel* originally was a servant, a person of lesser importance who entertained kings and noblemen.

Word Exploration Ideas

Assign your class the task of planning a *menu* entirely of *minced* dishes. Students may wish to prepare their favorite recipes to share.

The *minimum* wage is a current hot topic of conversation. Discuss with students the relationship between the minimum wage and the number of jobs available for teens.

How have religious *ministers* helped to shape American thought? Assign independent research on any of the following: Dr. Martin Luther King, Jr., Roger Williams, Mary Baker Eddy, Joseph Smith, Dwight L. Moody, Sojourner Truth, Malcolm X, Dr. Norman Vincent Peale.

Discuss the legal pros and cons of being a *minor*. Invite someone involved with your state's criminal justice system to explain the rights and privileges granted to children. What indicates adulthood? At what age are voting, driving, and working privileges permitted?

Challenge baseball fans to explain to the class the *minor* league system. What are the different classifications? How do the minor teams work with the major league teams?

READING FOR MEANING
-MIN-
small, less

What's on today's **menu**, Rootster?

The Vocab Cafe is serving up **minuscule** bites of macaroni **minuet**, a lively pasta that dances on the tongue! We also have **minced** mushrooms, a delightful plate of finely chopped fungi. For **minors** and adults desiring a **minimum** amount of food, Chef Rootster recommends the Pee Wee Platter, a **miniature** version of the full-sized meal.

After attending to dessert and other *minute* details, the Rootster whisks us off to Lexington, Massachusetts, to see the statue of the famous *Minuteman*. Our trusty tour guide explains that in the years before the American Revolution, *ministers* and other town leaders organized soldiers who were ready in a moment's notice to march against the British. So many men joined up that those who sided with England became a *minority.*

The tuneful Rootster reminds us that *minstrels* have preserved the deeds of the minutemen in song. "Oh, the brave Minutemen, so quick to defend. . ," he warbles.

ROOTING FOR MEANING
-MIN-

Write definitions for the boldfaced words. Refer to a dictionary. Include the root meaning (small or less) in each definition.

Example: minor—a person less than an adult, a child

ROOTSTER'S -MIN- RIDDLES

Read the vocabulary riddles at the bottom of this page. Write the letter of the matching answer in each blank.

a. Because he wasn't one of the Minutemen
b. Min-u-et yet, or are you still dancing?
c. Minuscule fuel
d. "Who's on the menu tonight?"
e. A minor shiner
f. Because he lost his voice
g. The fewer newer chewers
h. "Gee, there's a wee flea on me!"
i. At a mince meet (mincemeat)
j. A sinister minister
k. Minute fruit
l. A minimum (mini mom)

_____ 1. What kind of gas does a tiny car use?

_____ 2. Why did the minstrel offer a big reward?

_____ 3. Where did the chopped raisins compete with the diced apples?

_____ 4. Why did it take George Washington an hour to put on his boots?

_____ 5. What do you call an evil government official?

_____ 6. What did Rootster's dog, Wag, say when a miniature blood-sucking bug bothered him?

_____ 7. Knock-knock. Who's there? Min. Min who?

_____ 8. What do you call a kid's black eye?

_____ 9. What do you call a short mother?

_____ 10. What did Tom Thumb pack in his lunchbox?

_____ 11. What did one hungry cannibal say to the other?

_____ 12. Bessie Babysitter ran a daycare center. One day, she cooked oatmeal for the babies, but she only had enough to feed a minority of them. "I'll give hotdogs to the other kids," she said, "and save this oatmeal for. . . ."

WORKING WITH
-MIN-
WORDS

Use this nonsense poem to answer the questions below.

Pig Number One went to market.
Pig Number Two danced at home.
Pig Number Three had roast beef.
Pig Number Four had almost none.
Pig Number Five sang Do-Re-Mi, all the way home.
Pig Number Six walked his puppy dog.
Pig Number Seven found a little frog.
Pig Number Eight played with dollhouse chairs.
Pig Number Nine said all the prayers.
Down came the jar with a loud Slam! Slam!
And Pig Number Ten ate all the jam.

1. Which pig did a minuet? _____

2. Which pig was a minstrel? _____

3. Which pig had a minuscule pet? _____

4. Which pig was a minister? _____

5. Which pig liked minced fruit made into a spread? _____

6. Which pig had meat on his menu? _____

7. Which pig did a minimum of traveling? _____

8. Which pig ate a minute amount of food? _____

9. Which pig cared for a minor? _____

10. Which pig played with miniature furniture? _____

-PORT- to carry, entrance

deportment	*portcullis*
import	*porter*
port	*portfolio*
portable	*portico*
portage	*reporter*
portal	*transportation*

Unit Kickoff

Stump students with a geography question. What do the following cities have in common: Norfolk, Virginia; Cherbourg, France; Rio de Janeiro, Brazil; Cape Town, South Africa; Montreal, Quebec? The cities are all *ports*, centers of *transportation* for their regions. The early history of man and the development of nations is largely the story of ports. The root word -PORT- has found its way into an assortment of modern words, all sharing the idea of carrying or finding an entrance. Prior to giving students the list of -PORT- words, see how many they can brainstorm on their own.

Word Exploration Ideas

Have students use an encyclopedia to discover how many *porticoes* the White House boasts. The answer is two, the North Portico, which is square-shaped and serves as the main entrance, and the curved South Portico.

Show slides of medieval castles and point out the *portcullis* on each. Challenge students to identify other important castle features.

Assign independent research on any of these newsworthy *reporters* and journalists: Nellie Bly, Walter Cronkite, Edward R. Murrow, John Peter Zenger, Ida M. Tarbell, Samuel Hopkins Adams, Ernie Pyle, Margaret Bourke-White.

Today, manufacturers know that one good way to boost sales on a familiar product is to make it *portable*. What portable products, new or revamped, can your students design?

Provide topographical maps and direct students to plan a canoe trip complete with *portages*, rest stops, and supply lists. Scouts among your group may be able to suggest packing techniques to lighten the load during a portage.

Stockbrokers recommend that their clients maintain balanced *portfolios*. Invite an investment counselor to class to explain the basics of stocks, bonds, mutual funds, and commodities. Keep tabs on the stock reports in your local newspaper for a few days and ask students to develop lists of companies they would choose to add to a portfolio.

READING FOR MEANING
-PORT-
to carry, entrance

Hey, Rootster, is that a castle down there?

Our bumpy ride across the Atlantic calls for cool-headed **deportment**. Captain Rootster points out the emergency **portals**, in case we need to exit promptly.

But the danger passes, and our plucky pilot plunges down for a closer look. Beneath us lies Castle Caernarfon, built on a protected **port** in Wales. The **portcullis** gleams in the sunlight, still solid after centuries. A passenger comments on the massive stones used for the walls and **porticoes**. "Those blocks don't look very **portable** to me. How ever did they **import** them?"

Across the channel lies Anglesey, an island that depended on Caernarfon for supplies. A **reporter** on board opens his map **portfolio** to calculate the distance. "Phew!" he whistles. "I'd hate to be a castle **porter** back then. After crossing the water, they **transported** all cargo on foot. It was quite a **portage**!"

ROOTING FOR MEANING
-PORT-

Write definitions for the boldfaced words. Refer to a dictionary. Include a root meaning (to carry, entrance) in each definition.

Example: reporter—person who carries news back to his audience

ROOTSTER'S -PORT- RIDDLES

Oh, no! Someone has scrambled all of Rootster's -PORT- riddles! Write the letter of the correct answer beside each question.

_____ 1. What do you call a portfolio full of portraits?

_____ 2. What do you call a door that is alive?

_____ 3. What did the minister call his portable wedding chapel?

_____ 4. What do you call a small merchant of foreign products?

_____ 5. Which bird is known for its admirable deportment?

_____ 6. What is it called when you carry goods across a Caribbean island?

_____ 7. What is a light for a portico?

_____ 8. Two men were on a long portage. Finally, one turned to the other and said . . .

_____ 9. What did the puny porter say about the stuffed suitcase?

_____ 10. What did the evil knight say when he got caught in the portcullis?

_____ 11. What did the big harbor call the little harbor?

a. "Sneaking into this castle is a hassle!"

b. A porch torch

c. A behavin' raven

d. "I can't go another mile, can-oe?"

e. "Carry 'n' Marry"

f. A face case

g. The Mortal Portal

h. A shorter importer

i. Shorty-Port

j. Haitian transportation

k. "This carrier can't carry 'er!"

WORKING WITH
-PORT-
WORDS

deportment	portage	portfolio
import	portal	portico
port	portcullis	reporter
portable	porter	transportation

Use the vocabulary words from this unit to fill in the blanks in the list of rules below.

A _____'s Rules of _____

1. When delivering fiddles to Old King Cole, be extremely polite to the guard at the _____. There's no sense in getting caught in a tight squeeze!

2. Never drop Vincent Van Goat's _____ in a puddle. You may think a little mud improves his paintings, but he is likely to become very cross!

3. Never leave pizza on the _____ at Little Red Riding Hood's house. The neighborhood wolves might gobble it up!

4. Wear good walking shoes when you work for the Gently Down the Stream Canoe Company. First it's row, row, row, but soon it's _____, _____, _____!

5. Don't ever haul anything for a hog farmer. The only _____pig is a ham sandwich!

6. Don't force pumpkins through narrow _____ unless you especially like pie!

7. Before you deliver English curds and whey to Little Miss Muffet, check for spiders. You don't want to _____ any foreign pests!

8. When Blackbeard's ship sails into _____, you can be sure there will be plenty of work. Just don't go snooping around his treasure chests!

9. "Rub-a-dub-dub. Three men in a TUB?" Always choose the means of _____ best suited for the items you are carrying.

10. Don't talk about secret deliveries you have been hired to make. Save that job for the detectives and the _____. He who hauls and walks away gets hired to haul another day!

-GENS- a people, a kind

degenerate
eugenics
gendarme
gender
genealogy
generation
generic

gentleman
genuine
indigenous
ingenious
progeny
regenerate

Unit Kickoff

To introduce the -GENS- words, duplicate copies of a family tree chart and challenge students to fill in as many relatives' names as possible. Have the students count how many generations are shown. Use the charts in class as a springboard for discussing the meaning common to all the unit words, the idea of being born into a people, a race, or a kind. Then, let each student take his or her chart home to foster discussion of the family's **genealogy**. To what different locations has each family's **progeny** spread?

Word Exploration Ideas

Play a classroom version of the popular television show "The Price Is Right" to demonstrate the concept of **generic** versus brand-name products.

Encourage independent learning about **regeneration**. Which members of the animal kingdom show the most regenerative abilities? (Sponges, flatworms, starfish, glass lizards, crayfish, salamanders.) What limited regeneration occurs in most mammals, including humans? (hair, nails, skin)

Invite an animal breeder to speak on **eugenics**, selective breeding. Most people accept the practice in show animals and plants, but object to a human application, such as Hitler attempted.

Has the Age of the **Gentleman** passed? As a class project, write rules for conduct for gentlemen and ladies of the twenty-first century. What situations will you need to consider that etiquette books from the past never addressed?

Tell the students that the root -GENS- has produced many other words in addition to those in this unit, such as *antigen, congeniality, generator, generous, genesis, genetics, genie, genius, genocide, gentile.*

READING FOR MEANING
-GENS-
a people, a kind

Rootster, we have been in this plane for **generations**! We will **degenerate** into jellyfish if we do not land somewhere soon!

Our pleasant pilot, always the **gentleman**, calms our fears. Soon the plane touches down. "No **generic** sights today, folks," Rootster says. "We are in Australia, where the **indigenous** animals can trace their **genealogies** back 200 million years. That is when the Australian land mass pulled away and began to **regenerate**. With the principle of **eugenics** at work, the **progeny** of common mammals adapted to the land in **ingenious** ways."

"Take the platypus and the echidna, for example. Those of the female **gender** are the only **genuine** mammals anywhere in the world to hatch their young from eggs."

We tumble from the plane, eager to experience the unique wildlife. But Rootster's last words linger in our ears. "Look and enjoy, but do not interfere. These animals are protected by law so that future **generations** of Australians can enjoy them."

ROOTING FOR MEANING
-GENS-

Write definitions for the boldfaced words. Refer to a dictionary. Include a root meaning (a people, a kind) in each definition.

Example: progeny—offspring of one's own kind, children

ROOTSTER'S -GENS- RIDDLES

Read the vocabulary riddles below. Write the letter of the matching answer in each blank.

_____ 1. What do you do when you need an impressive genealogy?

_____ 2. What do you call a surgeon who treats either men or women but not both?

_____ 3. A visiting Martian asked his host to show him the life forms indigenous to Earth. What did his host say?

_____ 4. What do you call a family reunion?

_____ 5. What do you call the science of breeding better female sheep?

_____ 6. Who wrote the book *Tales of Genuine Swine*?

_____ 7. A waiter stopped a country boy from entering a restaurant. "Sir, the sign says, 'Gentlemen need jackets.' " What did the country boy say?

_____ 8. What do you call a town filled with progeny?

_____ 9. A scientist invented a way to sell fancy weather, like Philadelphia Phog or Purple Glo Sno. A worried farmer called up and said, "I need something cheap and generic. Do you have any_____?"

_____ 10. What do you call a march for degenerates?

_____ 11. Who wrote the book *From Leftovers to Clever Casseroles*?

_____ 12. A computer scientist named Jenner discovered he was dying of a mysterious illness. He asked his computer what he should do. What did the computer say?

_____ 13. Who wrote the book *Gendarme Alarm* ?

A. "Come on, I will show you the local yokels."

B. Plain Jane Rain

C. Ima Real Hogg

D. "I don't need a jacket. I'm not a gentleman."

E. Go on a family-tree shopping spree

F. A downgrade parade

G. A gender mender

H. N. Gene Yus

I. Ewe-genics

J. A generation celebration

K. "Re-Jenner-ate"

L. Kiddie City

M. C. D. Robber

WORKING WITH -GENS- WORDS

degeneration	genealogy	genuine
eugenics	generation	indigenous
gendarme	generic	ingenious
gender	gentleman	progeny
		regeneration

It's Rhyme Time! Use your knowledge of the unit words to fill in the blanks below.

1. Georgie Porgie Pudding 'n' Pie did not act like a _____. Those girls needed a _____ defender!

2. Mary Mary Quite Contrary was grouchy, but she certainly was an _____ gardener. Many different plants were _____ to her garden.

3. Jack and Jill is a poem about two children and their nasty _____.

4. The Old Woman Who Lived in the Shoe had so many _____, she didn't know what to do.

5. Wee Willie Winkie served as the sleep police of Mother Goose Land. He was a _____ gentle _____.

6. Diddle Diddle Dumpling's son always wore socks to bed. Perhaps he learned this odd habit from the previous _____.

7. "Jack Sprat could eat no fat. / His wife could eat no lean. / So when their little baby came, / He ate stuff in-between." This rhyme shows the principles of _____ at work. Little Baby Sprat has an interesting _____!

8. "There was a young star of the sea who lived very dangerously.
   He cut off an arm, but it did little harm,
   For it grew back as quick as could be."

   This rhyme deals with the natural phenomenon of _____.

9. "A grocery store owner named Hopper,
   Gave good advice to each shopper.
   'Don't judge by a name; they taste almost the same,
   So you might as well save on your copper.' "

   Mr. Hopper believes in buying _____ products.

-VID-, -VIS- to see, to look

evidence	*visage*
improvise	*vision*
invisible	*visionary*
provide	*visit*
revision	*visor*
supervise	*visual*
visa	*visualize*

Unit Kickoff

A supply of paper painters' hats will get your students thinking about the words in this unit. The hats, which can be obtained from a paint store at very low cost (or even donated, if you are lucky), have a *visor* suitable for embellishment. Pass out the hats and ask the students to add decorations that provide *evidence* of their personality traits. Display a sample to help students *visualize* the finished product.

Word Exploration Ideas

Take snapshots of your students to mount on a bulletin board titled *A Variety of **Visages** at _____ School*. If you use the kick-off idea described above, you may prefer to photograph students in their wacky hats and call the display *Visages in Visors*.

Tell your students that a *visa* is an official document that allows a person to travel within the country that issued it. Ask the students to suggest reasons that countries might want to restrict travel by unauthorized foreigners. If you have a visa, show it to the students.

At the heart of every good mystery novel is *evidence*—circumstantial, irrefutable, or lack of. Direct students to write down three pieces of evidence and then exchange lists with a partner. The partner creates a mystery plotline based on the evidence. This activity may uncover the next Sherlock Holmes!

Give your class comedians a moment in the spotlight. Stage a mini-production of "Live at the Improv Theater." Give each group of students a strip of paper on which you have written a humorous situation. Ask the group members to *improvise* the situation.

Ask the students what they think it means to *supervise* people. Encourage them to think of characteristics that a good supervisor might possess.

On the chalkboard, list the names of people who have been regarded as great *visionaries*—Leonardo da Vinci, Galileo, Columbus, Woodrow Wilson, Franklin D. Roosevelt, Edward Jenner, Louis Pasteur. Encourage students to read biographies of people such as these.

Name _____

READING FOR MEANING
-VID-, -VIS-
to see, to look

Rootster, where will our next **visit** take us?

Check your **visas** and adjust your **visors**, Vocab-Travelers. We are heading back to the Western Hemisphere—to one of the greatest theme parks ever! The **visual** delights of this famous park **provide** ample **evidence** that the park's creator was a great **visionary**.

The creator of this park **visualized** some unique ways to handle large numbers of people. When he offered his ideas to city planners, they simply laughed, so he built his own city and **supervised** every detail. In his park, he wanted maintenance to be **invisible**, so it would be done early in the morning before guests arrived. Transportation around the park was to be pleasant and convenient. When existing rail systems proved to be unsuitable, this visionary **improvised** one of his own.

After years of work, the **vision** was reality. When the park opened its gates to the public, hundreds of happy **visages** told the story and forced critics to **revise** their opinions.

ROOTING FOR MEANING
-VID-, -VIS-

Write definitions for the boldfaced words. Refer to a dictionary. Include a root meaning (to see, to look) in each definition.
Example: visualize—to see in one's mind, to imagine

ROOTSTER'S **-VID-**, **-VIS-** RIDDLES

The answers to some of Rootster's wacky vocabulary riddles are listed below. Write the number of the matching question beside each one.

_____ A. Invisi-Bull
_____ B. Goofy proof
_____ C. "If at first you don't succeed, improvise!"
_____ D. A visionary canary
_____ E. Visualize size
_____ F. Collision revision
_____ G. An outer-space face
_____ H. Provide-A-Ride
_____ I. 20/20/20
_____ J. "I always wanted to be the ring leader!"
_____ K. "Am I a sight or a vision?"
_____ L. A super visor for a supervisor
_____ M. A whizz-it visit
_____ N. A Pisa-visa

1. What is a good name for a carpool service?

2. What do you call wacky evidence?

3. What kind of present did the workers give their boss?

4. What is the best thing a short basketball player can do?

5. What do you call a passport to see the famous European leaning tower?

6. What is the name of an invention that farmers can get to keep strangers out of their fields?

7. What do you call a visage from the interplanetary regions?

8. A phone company worker was promoted to supervisor. What did she say about her new job?

9. What's perfect vision for a Martian?

10. What do you call a bird with big plans?

11. What do you call an extremely fast trip?

12. Why did the stunt drivers on the movie set groan? Because the director called for a _____.

13. What is the motto of the Spur-of-the-Moment Invention Company?

14. What did the woman trying on fancy hats say to her husband?

WORKING WITH
-VID-, -VIS-
WORDS

Rootster has cranked up the Wacky-Word-Maker Machine! This machine mixes up parts of words to make new ones. Match each nonsense word that Rootster has created to the definition that fits it.

_____ 1. improvise + visual = improvisual
_____ 2. revision + visionary = revisionary
_____ 3. provide + evidence = proevidence
_____ 4. supervise + visit = supervisit
_____ 5. invisible + visor = invisivisor
_____ 6. evidence + visage = evivisage
_____ 7. invisible + visualize = invisualize
_____ 8. decision + visionary = decisionary
_____ 9. benefit + visual = benevisual
_____10. improvise + vision = improvision
_____11. vocabulary + vision = vocavision
_____12. genealogy + visage = genevisage
_____13. revision + visa = revisa
_____14. minute + visit = minivisit
_____15. invisible + visa = invisa

a. a bill for a cap that cannot be seen
b. a spur-of-the-moment dream
c. a secret passport, one not seen by the naked eye
d. a person who sees what needs to be changed
e. a person who sees what must be decided
f. to oversee a trip
g. a travel document permitting a second trip back to a place
h. changing the appearance of something on the spur of the moment
i. proof written all over one's face
j. having the ability to put a dream into words
k. proof that you are supplying another's need
l. a very brief trip
m. to see what others cannot see
n. the face inherited from one's ancestors
o. seeing what would be the best for another

-SCRIB-, -SCRIP- to write

conscription	*scribe*
describe	*scripts*
inscription	*scripture*
manuscript	*scrivener*
prescription	*subscribe*
scribble	*transcribe*
	transcript

Unit Kickoff

With the help of some simple props, direct students in a mini-dramatization of "Rootster's Famous Moments in **-SCRIB-, -SCRIP-** History." The first actor needs a bathrobe and a quill pen for the activities of a medieval *scribe*, working away at a *manuscript* in a monastery. The second actor needs a visor, a pen, and a bottle of ink for his work as a nineteenth-century *scrivener*. The third actor uses a computer keyboard for his/her work as a modern-day *transcriber* of electronic records. Explain to students that the study of vocabulary is also the study of history. As the methods of writing have changed through the years, so have the words we use to name them.

Word Exploration Ideas

If possible, display pictures or reproductions of an old illuminated *manuscript*. Tell the students that an illuminated page is adorned with a fancy alphabet letter at the beginning of text or with other decorative designs. Provide paper and colored pencils so students can design decorative letters similar to those that might have appeared in old manuscripts.

Discuss the history of *scripture*, beginning with oral tradition and on to the written word.

Show your students an official school *transcript*. Have students discuss the type of data that goes on a transcript and think about ways that colleges and employers would use the information.

Invite a veteran to class to discuss *conscription* with your students. Later, survey students to find out if they think men and women should be drafted.

With your students, discuss some of the problems that plague your school. Direct students to write *prescriptions* that will help solve the problems. Post the prescriptions on a bulletin board titled *Just What Dr. Rootster Ordered: Prescriptions for a Better School."*

READING FOR MEANING
-SCRIB-, -SCRIP-
to write

Hey, Rootster! A giant lady is pointing at us!

Our pilot and official *scribe* looks up from the *manuscript* he is *scribbling*. He lands the plane on a tiny island that can only be *described* as trashy. Candy wrappers and soda cans are piled at the base of the famous Statue of Liberty. "This is just what the doctor ordered," Rootster chuckles. "The Great Lady pointed to us for a reason. She was *conscripting* us for emergency trash-relief!"

We pile out of the plane and begin picking up trash. We are glad to be improving the area so that visitors will describe the statue as an awesome sight, not a trash dump. "I hope this community service will go on my *transcript*," a student thought. "Many colleges *subscribe* to the idea that community service helps students become better all-around citizens."

Just then another student discovers the *inscription* on the base of the statue. "Give me your tired, your poor. . ." The famous words are almost as familiar as *Scripture*. The *scrivener* in our group grabs a pencil. He plans to *transcribe* copies of the inscription to give as souvenirs.

ROOTING FOR MEANING
-SCRIB-, -SCRIP-

Write definitions for the boldfaced words. Refer to a dictionary. Include the root meaning (to write) in each definition.

Example: subscribe—to write one's name beneath; to place an order by signing

ROOTSTER'S -SCRIB-, -SCRIP- RIDDLES

Oh, no! Someone has scrambled all of Rootster's -SCRIB-,-SCRIP- riddles! Write the letter of the correct answer beside each question.

_____ 1. What are the two best words in an awful movie script?

_____ 2. What is the name of the exciting new game where the person with the worst penmanship wins?

_____ 3. Who wrote *The Do-It-Yourself Guide to Prescriptions*?

_____ 4. What did one scrivener say to the other?

_____ 5. Joe: Moe, did you know that some of the early scriptures were written on leather?
Moe:_____

_____ 6. To what publication did King Tut subscribe?

_____ 7. Where do the animals of the forest go when they need inscriptions done?

_____ 8. What grades were recorded on the sleepy student's transcript?

_____ 9. What did the frustrated scribe call his new book?

_____ 10. What is the best way to put the big squeeze on an enemy?

_____ 11. First scuba diver: How would you describe that electric eel swimming right behind you?
Second scuba diver: _____

a. "Holy Cow!"
b. The engravin' raven
c. *The Ripped Manuscript*
d. Conscript a boa constrictor.
e. The End
f. Scribble
g. R. U. Sik
h. "Don't copy me!"
i. Mummy Monthly
j. Z-Z-Zs
k. "In glowing terms!"

WORKING WITH
-SCRIP, -SCRIB-
WORDS

Yipes! Rootster is walking through a graveyard, reading tombstones! Match each inscription with the letter of the correct person.

_____ 1. Words cannot describe him but he is speechless at last.
_____ 2. Eternally out of ink, I think.
_____ 3. If only that prescription hadn't been scribbled!
_____ 4. She reached the end of her final season.
_____ 5. The final curtain's going up. No more script changes for me.
_____ 6. Once I subscribed to *Life*. Is it too late to renew?
_____ 7. Does this go on my permanent transcript?
_____ 8. The scripture is a true picture.
_____ 9. Hand done.
_____ 10. From the Book of Life into the Book of Death—I have been transcribed.
_____ 11. The Egyptians' inscriptions gave me fatal conniptions!

   a. A television script writer
   b. A man who died reading sacred writings
   c. A scribe
   d. A famous public speaker
   e. A magazine reader
   f. A manuscript writer
   g. An old scrivener
   h. A student who died trying a crazy stunt
   i. An archeologist who died translating hieroglyphics
   j. A patient who took the wrong medicine
   k. A playwright

Write some witty tombstone inscriptions of your own using the unit words.
Here are some ideas to get you started.
   • a soldier who died dodging the draft
   • a teacher who died trying to read students' scribbles
   • a magazine publisher
   • a doctor
   • an engraver of tombstones

-NOM-, -NYM- name

anonymous	*namesake*	*renown*
antonym	*nom de plume*	*surname*
cognomen	*nomenclature*	*synonym*
denomination	*nominate*	
misnomer	*pseudonym*	

Unit Kickoff

Create instant interest in the words of this unit by waving a fistful of play money before your students. Give a brief money quiz in which you ask questions about the faces on the different bill and coin **denominations**.

$1.00—George Washington	penny—Abraham Lincoln
$5.00—Abraham Lincoln	nickel—Thomas Jefferson
$10.00—Alexander Hamilton	dime—Franklin D. Roosevelt
$20 00—Andrew Jackson	quarter—George Washington
	half-dollar—John F. Kennedy

Word Exploration Ideas

Have your students identify the author for each of these **noms de plume**.
 Mark Twain (Samuel L. Clemens)
 Dr. Seuss (Theodor Seuss Geisel)
 O. Henry (William Sydney Porter)
 James Herriot (J. A. Wright)
 Lewis Carroll (Charles Dodson)
 Ellery Queen (Frederic Dannay & Manfred B. Lee)

Challenge students to create a dictionary that teachers and parents everywhere need—*Guide to Middle School* **Nomenclature**. Suggest that students include current terms about fashion, sports, music, and so on.

Send students home to explore the history of their **surnames**. Many last names derive from place names, occupations, or physical descriptions.

Locate a copy of **Anonymous** *Was a Woman*, by Mirra Bank. Encourage your students to browse through the book. The author's purpose in writing the book was to examine art by unknown female folk artists and to make their lives less of a mystery.

Have students build **synonym** word chains. The last letter in one word must be the first letter in the following word, as in *beautiful* and *lovely.*

READING FOR MEANING
-NOM-, -NYM-
name

> All aboard, gang! We are off to Paris, France, the home of another great lady!

The passengers on Rootster's plane try to guess the identity of our mystery lady. We **nominate** several **surnames**, but our Vocab-Master shakes his head. "She is world **renowned**, but to call her by a real name is a **misnomer**. We are certain of her **nom de plume**, but she herself is **anonymous**. Today we are traveling to Paris because that is where her first book was published in 1697. A French writer, Charles Perrault, wrote down eight of her stories that were of the folk tale **denomination**. He titled them *Tales of My Mother Goose.*"

Rootster continues, "The **pseudonym** Monsieur Perrault created quickly became **synonymous** for any literature written for small children. The good Mother Goose has had many **namesakes** through the years. Each has used the characteristics that children everywhere love—talking animals, silly people, rhyming words, **antonyms**, and twisting syllables. Let's try to think of a suitable **cognomen** for a modern-day writer of children's stories or rhymes."

ROOTING FOR MEANING
-NOM-, -NYM-

Write definitions for the boldfaced words. Refer to a dictionary. Include the root meaning (name) in each definition.

Example: antonym—a word that names the opposite

ROOTSTER'S -NOM-, -NYM- RIDDLES

Gosh! These riddles are almost finished, but Rootster has left out some important words. Fill in the blanks with words that will complete the idea of each riddle.

antonym　　　*Nominate*　　　*Unknown*
Nomer　　　*Nom de plume*　　　*Pseudonym*
Worm　　　*Synonym*　　　*Too*
Denominator　　　*Surname*　　　*Bubble*
Famous

1. Who is a chocolate chip cookie baker of world renown? _____ Amos

2. What did the museum name the antique chair given by an anonymous donor? The
_____ Throne

3. What do you call a contest of cognomens?　The _____ Game

4. What do you call nomenclature that deals with caterpillars, maggots, and nightcrawlers?
_____ Terms

5. "Synonym adds such nice flavor to applesauce," said Miss _____

6. Have you read the new book by Will E. Run? It's called *Whom Shall We* _____

7. What do you call an evil assumed name?　A Grim _____

8. Why did Mother Goose pluck out all her feathers? She was searching for a good

_____

9. What bath product has a foamin' cognomen?　Mr. _____

10. What do you call a person who dislikes working with fractions?
A _____ Hater

11. What do you call another word for slender, slight, and skinny? A Slim _____

12. What did people call Mr. Mee's namesake?　Mee, _____!

13. What do you call a song in praise of opposites?　An _____Hymn

Name _____

WORKING WITH
-NOM-, -NYM-
WORDS

Rootster says, "Here's a story told to me by the writer, May I. Sing, better known in China as Auntie Quack-Quack. Read the story; then answer the questions below."

Long ago in a magical city, a young woman named Shy Pearl ran a well-known restaurant with help from seven servants. Their names were Snuggle, Snore, Sigh, Whisper, Yawn, Ah-Choo, and Ah-Choo, Jr. They all belonged to the High Order of Helpful Enchanted Beings, and each day the restaurant was filled with happiness. People came from all around to eat Shy Pearl's food. But in the house next door, all was not well. The wizard who lived there, High-Fat, belonged to the High Order of Evil Enchanted Beings. He also had seven servants, and he never gave them enough to eat. Every night, Shy Pearl heard their pitiful cries of hunger.

Finally, Shy Pearl decided to secretly send over some food for High-Fat's hungry servants to eat. She thought about which of her servants to send. "Not Whisper," she thought. "He is the loudest of all. I'll send Yawn. He knows many names and magic words to use in case High-Fat catches him."

Late that night, Yawn tiptoed next door, carrying a basket of Shy Pearl's famous tofu burgers. But High-Fat awoke and asked in an angry voice, "Who is disturbing my household?"

"It is only I, your faithful servant, Itsy Bitsy," Yawn said. "I have locked the leftovers from dinner in the cupboard so those greedy brothers of mine won't eat them." With that, High-Fat went back to sleep, and Yawn successfully delivered Shy Pearl's burger basket to the seven hungry servants.

1. What was the evil wizard's cognomen? _____

2. Which servant had a namesake? _____

3. Who was a cook of great renown? _____

4. Who used a nom de plume? _____

5. Which servant was good with nomenclature? _____

6. What is a synonym for Snuggle's name? _____

7. Which of Shy Pearl's servants had a name that was a misnomer? _____

8. To which magical denomination did High-Fat belong? _____

9. Whom did Shy Pearl nominate for the delivery job? _____

10. What is an antonym for High-Fat's name? _____

-MITT-, -MISS- to send

admit
commissary
commitment
committee
intermittent
message

missile
missionary
missive
permission
remittance
smitten
submissive

Unit Kickoff

Label some paper airplanes with words from this unit. Sail them across the room with the explanation that they all are *missiles*, objects sent through the air. Examine the prefixes, suffixes, and participles included in the list and how they refine the root meaning, to send. *Admit* is to send into; *permission* is the act of sending through; *smitten* is the passive participle of smite, to deliver a blow. Challenge students to design their own airplanes that show (through sentences, synonyms, or drawings) the meanings of individual words from the list.

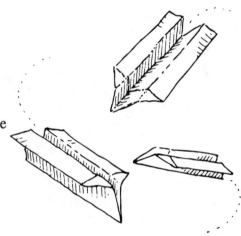

Word Exploration Ideas

Is *commitment* a strong value in today's culture? See if students can add to this starter list of formal and informal pledges or commitments: marriage vows, a promise to a friend, a courtroom oath, a school honor code, the Pledge of Allegiance to the American flag, scouting oaths, a handshake.

Enlist student actors to role-play situations that demonstrate the pros and cons of *submissiveness*. When is being submissive a positive quality? When is it undesirable?

Launch a flurry of *missive*-writing in your classroom! The addresses below are excellent sources of age-appropriate pen pals for your students.

Worldwide Friendship International
3749 Brice Run Road, Station A
Randallstown, MD 21133

World Pen Pals
1694 Como Ave.
St. Paul, MN 55108

Today, we use fax machines for instant communication, but in its era, Morse code was revolutionary. Provide copies of the *intermittent* dot-dash code so students can try their hand at sending messages in this manner.

READING FOR MEANING
-MITT-, -MISS-
to send

Rootster, are those underwater **missiles**?

Intermittent streaks of gray pass through the waves beneath the plane. Our pilot lowers the landing gear and we exit, feeling like *missionaries* on a deserted island. There are no crowds, no welcoming *committees*, just hot sun, blue sea, and those moving shapes in the water. Could we be in the Caribbean?

"You are correct," Rootster *admits*. "This is tiny Cayman Brac, and those creatures in the water are sting rays. Come on, gang. We have *permission* to feed them."

Our world-traveling wordsmith heads for a tiny *commissary* hidden under the palm trees. For a small *remittance*, he buys a bag of bait and wades out in the water. "Don't be afraid," he calls. "The rays are very *submissive*. See?" We make a *commitment* to follow, despite our jitters.

The great creatures rush to rub against us, sending silent, friendly *messages*. *Smitten*, we carefully feed them. "Wait until the folks back home read tonight's *missive*," someone mutters. "They'll never believe I fed a live sting ray!"

ROOTING FOR MEANING
-MITT-, -MISS-

Write definitions for the boldfaced words. Refer to a dictionary. Include the root meaning (to send) in each definition.

Example: committee—a group sent to meet together

ROOTSTER'S -MITT-, -MISS- RIDDLES

Read the vocabulary riddles below. Write the letter of the matching answer in each blank.

_____ 1. A minister moved to a foreign country to preach. He got so busy, he did not have time to get a haircut. What did his new friends call him?

_____ 2. What do you call a crazy torpedo that hits its target only half the time?

_____ 3. What do you call a message thrown out of a volcano?

_____ 4. What do you call a meeting of ants?

_____ 5. Mother Rabbit ran out of fruit while making jam, so she sent Peter to the store. Where did he go?

_____ 6. What do you call an intermittent stoplight at a smelly trash dump?

_____ 7. The missive-writer was in a big hurry. What did he say to the mailman?

_____ 8. What do you call a young tomcat hit with a bad case of puppy love?

_____ 9. What do you call a commitment made at the top of a cliff?

_____ 10. What is the name of that quiet new sport where the players are all very submissive?

_____ 11. What kind of hand covering allows you to enter any locked door?

_____ 12. A town by the sea installed a public shower for all the tourists who came to swim. When you made your remittance, the water came on automatically. What did the townspeople call their shower?

_____ 13. A boy tossed a penny into the king's magic well. "Oh, well," he said, "give me a new bike." What did the well say?

    a. News of the ooze
    b. The Tame Game
    c. "Deliver de letter, de sooner, de better!"
    d. Their hairy missionary
    e. Admittens
    f. A stinker blinker
    g. A hit-or-missile
    h. An itty bitty committee
    i. The Berry Commissary
    j. A smitten kitten
    k. "Young man, do you have the king's wishin' permission?"
    l. A pledge on the edge
    m. Pay and Spray

WORKING WITH
-MITT-, -MISS-
WORDS

admit	missionary
commissaries	missives
commitment	permission
committee	remittance
intermittent	smitten
messages	submissive
missile	

Use the vocabulary words from this unit to fill in the blanks in the advertisement below.

Introducing an exciting new magazine that is out-of-this-world!

Better Homes and Planets

Are you (1)_____ by the stars? Do you dream of being a

(2)_____ to another world? Would you like to browse through the two famous

(3)_____, Asteroids-R-Us and MoonMart? Now at last, you can

(4)_____ it. Like thousands of other readers, you are fascinated with Extraterrestrial Life.

This new publication (5)_____ you to enjoy the enchantment of Saturn without ever

leaving home. Read thrilling (6)_____ sent in by our Martian correspondents.

(7)_____ yourself to Plutonian beauty treatments that pamper mind and body. See

how (8)_____ lightning bolts can give your home that flashy, Outer-Space look.

Learn how to turn old (9)_____ parts into dis-arming coffee tables. Don't spend

another day without Better Homes and Planets! Make a (10)_____ to

send in your (11)_____ today!

Subscribe now and receive as our free gift to you, (12)_____ from the Milky Way,

a lively recording of satellite signals by Daddy Big Dipper and the Comets. Brought to you by

C.O.M.A, the (13)_____ on Martian Adventure.

Wait 'til you see what's out there!
It's all in the pages of *Better Homes and Planets*.

Write an article for this exciting new magazine. Use as many of the unit words as you can.

-CHRON-, -TEMP- time

anachronism	*contemporary*
chronic	*extemporaneous*
chronicle	*synchronize*
chronology	*temper*
chronometer	*tempest*

Unit Kickoff

Divide your class into two groups. Challenge the group members to arrange themselves in **chronological** order by birthday. Keep time with a stopwatch so you can declare a winner. Next, give the same assignment but provide cards listing historical events. When the fun and confusion have died down, point out that the Greek root -CHRON- traces back to the Greek god, Cronus. The ancient Greeks used the movement of the sun in the sky as a way to measure the passing of time. -CHRON- and its Latin counterpart, -TEMP-, have found their way into many modern words.

Word Exploration Ideas

Use the arts to enrich the exploration of words. Display a copy of Salvadore Dali's surreal painting of melting **chronometers**, *The Persistence of Memory*. To encourage supplemental reading, share with your class the opening paragraphs of *The Martian Chronicles* by Ray Bradbury. Look for the **anachronisms** in *A Connecticut Yankee in King Arthur's Court* by Mark Twain.

Enlist the help of the musically inclined to lead a game of Simon Says, featuring these **tempo** terms: *accelerando, adagio, agitato, allegro, largo, prestissimo, presto, ritardando, vivace.* Be sure the student leaders explain the terms to the class before beginning the game.

Assign independent research on types of **tempests**—blizzards, cyclones, dust storms, hurricanes, monsoons, tornadoes. Some students may wish to explain the forces that cause the storms and others may wish to compile dates and statistics.

Provide practice in **extemporaneous** speaking by listing and numbering six school-related topics on the board. Have students roll a die to select a topic on which to speak. Include topics such as *My Best Teacher, The Food in the Cafeteria, The One School Rule I Would Change, The Most Important Thing I Have Learned in School.*

READING FOR MEANING
-CHRON-, -TEMP-
time

R-R-Rootster, are we going to make it through this s-s-storm?

We rub our *temples* as dark clouds surround the plane. Our captain of the sunny *temper* smiles. "Don't let this *tempest* scare you. Your *temporal* days aren't over yet! The skies around here are *chronically* cloudy."

Soon Rootster slows the *tempo* of the flight. He talks with his *contemporaries* in air traffic control. The clouds part *temporarily* and we catch a glimpse of the famed Big Ben of London. "Time to *synchronize* our *chronometers*," Rootster says.

Beside our digital watches and laptop computers, the tall clock tower with the giant bell seems like an *anachronism.* "On the contrary," our tour guide replies. "Big Ben's clock has accurately *chronicled* the passing of time for over 125 years."

As we adjust our personal timepieces, Rootster launches into an *extemporaneous chronology*. "In 1859, the bell rang from the tower for the first time. It was broadcast on the radio in 1923, and first appeared on TV in 1949 . . ."

ROOTING FOR MEANING
-CHRON-, -TEMP-

Write definitions for the boldfaced words. Refer to a dictionary. Include the root meaning (time) in each definition.

Example: contemporary—living in the same time, current

ROOTSTER'S -CHRON-, -TEMP- RIDDLES

The answers to some of Rootster's wacky vocabulary riddles are listed below. Write the number of the matching question beside each answer.

_____ A. A speedy-tweety

_____ B. I. Bluitt

_____ C. Synchronized scratching

_____ D. He wanted to read the headlines.

_____ E. A stormin' foreman

_____ F. Jess A. Minute

_____ G. She wanted to watch time fly.

_____ H. Buy-ology

_____ I. She liked to see order on the border.

_____ J. A chronic tonic

_____ K. Hugo Furst

_____ L. C. D. Church

_____ M. "Someone owes me a chronology apology."

_____ N. A temporary prairie

_____ O. *The Creepy Crawler Chronicles*

1. What do you call grassland that is not permanent?

2. Why did the girl glue feathers on her chronometer?

3. Who wrote the book *Giving an Extemporaneous Speech*?

4. Why did Wacky Wally examine his friend's temples?

5. What do you call a bird that flies at a quick tempo?

6. Who wrote the book *How to Control Your Temper*?

7. Two girls liked to shop for contemporary clothes. What did they call their hobby?

8. Who wrote the book *Great Temples of the World*?

9. What do you call a medicine you must take over and over?

10. What do you call a supervisor who gets caught out in a tempest?

11. Who wrote the book *Leaving This Temporal Life*?

12. What is the name of the worms' history book?

13. The name of the hottest new dance group is Poison Ivy. What do they call their routine?

14. The time machine goofed and sent the scientist to the wrong century. What did the scientist say?

15. Fussy Fran stopped the bus as it neared the state line. Why did she make the passengers line up chronologically by age?

WORKING WITH
-CHRON-,
-TEMP-
WORDS

anachronism	synchronize
chronic	temple
chronicle	temporal
chronology	temporary
chronometer	temper
contemporary	tempest
extemporaneous	tempo

K.I.S.S. is one of Rootster's favorite passwords. It means Keep It Simple, Silly! Can you rewrite each wordy sentence below in six words or less?

1. As a fan of music, I prefer current and up-to-date selections over those that previous generations enjoyed.

2. Put the lid on thoughts and emotions of an angry or passionate nature!

3. The sickly man suffered from an annoying ailment that frequently recurred most inconveniently.

4. The wind raged and howled; the waves crashed beneath the plane; the pilot could see no way around the wild and terrible storm.

5. Their solution to the problem would last for just a short period of time.

6. Each day, Anne Frank faithfully wrote out a detailed account of the events, large and small, that had occurred.

7. The flattened space on either side of his forehead was very sore to the touch, due to the severe nature of the headache he had endured.

8. If those of you who are playing musical instruments would be so kind as to accelerate the speed at which you are playing, I would greatly appreciate it.

9. The quick-witted president answered the reporter's surprise question with a five-minute explanation that was completely unprepared and unrehearsed.

10. The modern slang used by individuals playing historical roles on stage was chronologically incorrect.

11. It is not advisable to fill your minds solely with concerns over the impermanent details of life here on earth.

12. First the crystal cracked, then the hands stopped moving, and finally a spring from inside the chronometer flew out.

13. Both students reorganized their plans so that they ended up doing the same things at the same time each day.

14. The student wrote down the historical events in the wrong sequence.

-GEO-, -TERR- earth

extraterrestrial
geocentric
geodesic
geography
geology
geometry
internment

Mediterranean
subterranean
terrace
terra firma
terrain
territory

Unit Kickoff

Throw a tasting party and invite students to sample the bounty of the **Mediterranean** region. Provide olives, feta cheese, and pita bread as you discuss the twin roots, -GEO- and -TERR-. They come from ancient mythology; the Greek *Gaea* and the Latin *Terra* were the names given to the Mother Earth goddess. See how many words students can list on their own that are derived from these roots. Supplement the unit list with these derivatives:

terra cotta (baked earth)   geopolitics (global politics)
terra incognita (unknown country)   geothermal (earth's heat)
terrier (earth-digging dog)   terrarium (earth container)

Word Exploration Ideas

Challenge students to read up on the fascinating history of modern astronomy. For about 1,400 years, the **geocentrists**, led by the Greek astronomer Ptolemy, held the majority opinion. Then along came a heliocentrist, Nicolaus Copernicus, who theorized that every planet moved around the sun.

Provide toothpicks and rubber cement for a **geodesic dome** building activity.

What is the difference between a state and a **territory**? U.S. territories have no regular representation in Congress, but residents are guaranteed the same rights as American citizens. Display a world map so students can locate the following U.S. territories: the Virgin Islands, Guam, American Samoa, the Pacific Islands. (Although many people consider Puerto Rico and the Mariana Islands to be territories, they are actually U.S. commonwealths.)

Assign each student the task of mapping out a make-believe island, complete with **geographical** features and interesting **terrain**. Have each student write a paragraph describing what makes his or her **terra firma** the perfect place to live.

READING FOR MEANING
-GEO-, -TERR-
earth

Our trusty tour guide steps out on *terra firma* and surveys the desert *terrain*. "Think back on old *geography* lessons," he says. "We are near the *Mediterranean*, in the *territory* between the Tigris and Euphrates Rivers, home of ancient *geometric terraces* that towered 75 feet in the air. We need exercise, so we're going to see what *subterranean* secrets we can rescue from centuries of *internment*."

As Rootster passes out shovels, we realize we are in modern-day Iraq where the great hanging gardens of Babylon once stood. We dig at the ancient site until dark, battling against the sand and rocks that make up the *geology* of the area. One traveler says, "It seems as if we are at the very center of the universe."

"My, my! How *geocentric* of you!" Rootster chuckles.

ROOTING FOR MEANING
-GEO-, -TERR-

Write definitions for the boldfaced words. Refer to a dictionary. Include the root meaning (earth) in each definition.
Example: Mediterranean—having to do with the ocean in the mid-region of the earth

ROOTSTER'S -GEO-, -TERR- RIDDLES

Match the book titles on the left with the most logical author on the right.

_____ 1. *Earth at the Center of It All*

_____ 2. *Monsters of the Mediterranean*

_____ 3. *Trimming the Growth on Your Terrain*

_____ 4. *The Geography of a Place North of England*

_____ 5. *How to Avoid Unpleasant Internment Odor*

a. Berry M. Deep

b. Lon Moore

c. G.O. Sentrick

d. C. Serpent

e. Scott Land

For each riddle below, write the letter of the correct answer.

_____ 6. What is the favorite brand of bathroom tissue on Mars?

_____ 7. What did the geologist call his luxury car?

_____ 8. What did the explorer call the new country full of worms?

_____ 9. Where does a man-eating tiger live?

_____ 10. What do you call a lady who inherits a very nice porch?

_____ 11. What is another name for a subterranean sheep dog?

_____ 12. What did the elf call his geodesic house?

f. In gory territory
g. An underground hound
h. E.T.T.P. (Extraterrestrial Toilet Paper)
i. The domed gnome home
j. A terrace heiress
k. The rockin' Rolls
l. Terra Squirma

Choose one of the riddles above and draw a cartoon to illustrate it.

WORKING WITH
-GEO-, -TERR-
WORDS

Rootster has started a new business, the Bright Idea Invention Company. Match each clever product listed below with the correct description.

_____ 1. The Bigger Digger

_____ 2. Terrace Tennis

_____ 3. SONIC-ZOOM

_____ 4. Mediterranean Mattress

_____ 5. Rock Shock

_____ 6. Geographic Traffic

_____ 7. Invisa-Wall

_____ 8. Subterranean Spy

_____ 9. Pollution Palace

_____ 10. Geometry-Genius

_____ 11. Terrific-Terrain-Changer

_____ 12. Geocentric Drill

_____ 13. Terra-Firming Gel

a. An exciting new video game that lets you design roads that go everywhere. But be careful! There are car pile-ups and other dangers in all the countries you visit.

b. This enormous geodesic dome pops up to cover any environmental disaster area, before the contamination spreads. Keeps smog and odors in and clean air out.

c. One drop of this powerful formula dissolves drill-busting geologic matter.

d. This amazing new bulldozer makes quick work of internment. Scoops out coffin-shaped holes in 20 seconds.

e. Now you can eliminate ugly daytime fence lines! Stake out your territory with beams of reflective light, visible only at night.

f. This underground probe lets you look deep into the earth's layers to get to the core of the matter.

g. Use our incredibly quick tool to dig into the center of the earth. Brought to you by the makers of the Subterranean Spy.

h. The newest way to work on your swing without ever leaving your own back porch.

i. Eliminate quicksand with this amazing new formula.

j. A few squirts and you'll be extraterrestrial!

k. Guaranteed to bring you glorious dreams of the perfect oceanside vacation.

l. A computer program that will help you master crazy circles, troublesome triangles, and squeamish squares.

m. Dreaming of dunes? Crazy about canyons? Mooning over mountains? At last, you can select the type of land you want for your own backyard.

-JECT- to throw

conjecture   *jetsam*
dejected   *rejection*
injection   *project*
interjection   *trajectory*
jet   *subject*

Unit Kickoff

Get a game of classroom catch going with a ball of paper. Toss the ball to the first student and call out a common one-word *interjection,* such as *oh!* or *ugh!* As the student returns the ball to you, call out another interjection. Continue tossing the ball and saying interjections until the class gets the idea. Explain that the object of the game is to see how many different exclamations the students can think of without repeating themselves. Then have the sudents play the game with one another. Tell the students that an interjection is a word that expresses strong emotion (a word often thrown into the middle of a sentence or conversation). Present the remaining unit words and ask for *conjectures* as to their meanings. Guide students to use the idea of throwing in each guess that they make.

Word Exploration Ideas

Take your class outside on a mission—to collect litter from the campus. Analyze the findings. Why were the items discarded? What *conjectures* could an archeologist make upon finding this litter hundreds of years from now?

Author Madeleine L'Engle is living proof that *rejection* is never final. Share with the class this information about the publication of the Newbery-winning title, *A Wrinkle in Time.* Upon completing the book, Miss L'Engle began sending it to different publishers. Editor after editor rejected the book as being too unusual. After numerous negative responses, Miss L'Engle grew discouraged and decided to give up. A friend encouraged her to try one last publishing house, and her manuscript was finally accepted.

Send students to the library to compile a photo-history of the *jet* airplane. Have each student or group focus on a different model of jet aircraft.

Use this group of unit words to review common prefixes. Demonstrate how these prefixes affect the root meaning, to throw:

  injection - thrown in   object - to throw against
  interjection - thrown in between reject - to throw back
  project - to throw thoughts forward trajectory - to throw across
  subject - to throw under

READING FOR MEANING
-JECT-
to throw

*Attention, word travelers, this is your **jet** pilot speaking. From the **jetsam** beneath us, I **conjecture** that someone down there is in big trouble. Unless you **object**, I am going down for a closer look.*

Rootster skims over the sea, and soon we spot a ***dejected***-looking group of sailors huddled on a rock ***jetty***. The remains of their boat and the cargo they had ***jettisoned*** bob around in the rough waves.

Our courageous captain prepares to launch a ***projectile*** of emergency supplies. "Wait!" ***interjects*** one of the passengers, a doctor. He holds a medical bag full of pain-killing ***injections***. "Emergency treatment is one area I know very well. Send me down there!"

Rootster ***rejects*** this idea due to the danger. He proceeds to drop the rescue package. We anxiously watch its ***trajectory***. Will the package hit its target? Will the supplies help the sailors until a ship can pick them up?

ROOTING FOR MEANING
-JECT-

Write definitions for the boldfaced words. Refer to a dictionary. Include the root meaning (throw) in each definition.

Example: projectile—an object thrown through the air.

ROOTSTER'S -JECT- RIDDLES

This time, Rootster has rounded up a whole collection of those hilarious rhyming riddles known as hinky-pinkies. Match each hinky-pinky with the correct clue.

_____ 1. A gloomy roomie is . . .

_____ 2. A Nile projectile is . . .

_____ 3. A trash stash is . . .

_____ 4. A confection rejection is. . .

_____ 5. A petty jetty is . . .

_____ 6. A hot shot is . . .

_____ 7. A wrecked deck is . . .

_____ 8. Subterranean Spy

_____ 9. A dejected interjection is . . .

_____ 10. A yes guess is . . .

_____ 11. To jettison medicine is . . .

_____ 12. A tropic topic is . . .

_____ 13. A math path is . . .

a. a sad exclamation.

b. an uncomfortably warm injection.

c. the trajectory an algebra book takes when you slide it across the table.

d. the crocodile that Queen Cleopatra kicked across the river.

e. to send aid to sick fish.

f. a hidden pile of jetsam.

g. when your subject is Hawaii.

h. a dejected bunkmate.

i. a positive conjecture.

j. an airplane that flies into a rain cloud.

k. an allergic reaction from eating too much candy.

l. an object destroyed in a disaster.

m. a small and trivial ocean pier.

Name _____

WORKING WITH -JECT- WORDS

conjecture	jetsam	projectile
dejection	jettison	rejection
injection	jetty	subject
interjection	object	trajectory
jet		

Rootster wonders if you can you right these wrongs. Each sentence below uses a vocabulary word incorrectly. Cross out each incorrect word and write the correct word on the line.

1. The flu interjection I received at the doctor's office was very painful. _____

2. Fishing from a jet is lots of fun, but you have to be careful where you cast your line. _____

3. His mood of deep injection was due to the low grade he got on his project. _____

4. The camera caught in slow motion the jetsam of the pitcher's fastball. It was truly amazing. _____

5. The knight bowed low before his king. "Sir, I am your humble projectile." _____

6. At the first sign of engine trouble, the pilot and his crew rejected the excess baggage out the hatch. _____

7. The jetty was so heavy, only a weight-lifter could move it. _____

8. The sand was littered with dejection from the sinking ship. _____

9. The clown became a human interjection when he was shot from the cannon. _____

10. The whole family jettisoned about the contents of the mysterious package. _____

11. "No vulgar trajectories, please," said Miss Manners. "Remember, we are all ladies and gentlemen." _____

12. The object of gas released from the balloon sent it high into the clouds. _____

13. The conjecture of his marriage proposal hurt Hank so that he remained single for years. _____

-CARN-, -CORP- body

carnival
carnelian
carnage
carnation
carnivore
corpse
corporal

corpulent
corpuscle
corsage
corset
esprit de corps
incorporate
reincarnation

Unit Kickoff

Display photos of Michelangelo's work and point out the beautifully portrayed muscle and movement of the human body. Ask students to guess the role that *corpses* played in the artist's development. (Michelangelo's intimate knowledge of anatomy was gained partly through autopsies that he performed on corpses.)

How many other words derived from -CORP- and -CARN- can the students list?

Word Exploration Ideas

Challenge students to research and dramatize the role of red and white *corpuscles* in human blood. Red blood cells deliver oxygen from the heart and return carbon dioxide to be exhaled. The white corpuscles protect against infection and disease.

Invite your students to share their knowledge of common military ranks. What is the difference between officers and enlisted personnel? At what level is a *corporal*? Invite a local military recruiter to display military insignia and explain the various ranks.

Plan menus for the zoo! Assign students the task of listing appropriate foods for *carnivores*, herbivores, and omnivores. Remind the students to allocate enough food for the more *corpulent* animals.

READING FOR MEANING
-CARN-, -CORP-
body

Our plane lands. The noise on the ground is deafening. Grotesque faces crowd around our windows, like the **reincarnation** of a terrible nightmare. Rootster smiles at our frightened faces. "It's **carnival** time," he explains and passes out **corsages** for the ladies and red **carnations** for the men.

We are in New Orleans for Mardi Gras. Rootster directs us through the crowds toward a row of restaurants. "Attention **carnivores**, herbivores, and omnivores!" he shouts. "Here you will find enough food to suit your every desire."

A rather **corpulent** traveler smacks her lips and loosens her **corset**. "As you can see," Rootster continues, "the **espirit de corps** in this city is exhilarating. Meet me back here in one hour if you want to watch the parade. It will **incorporate** great music and fantastic costumes."

At midnight, the festival ends. We survey the **carnage** left behind—trash, bits of food, and cast-off costumes with **carnelian** pendants.

ROOTING FOR MEANING
-CARN-, -CORP-

Write definitions for the boldfaced words. Refer to a dictionary. Include the root meaning (body) in each definition.
Example: corpuscle—blood cell from a living body.

ROOTSTER'S -CARN-, -CORP- RIDDLES

Not again! Someone has scrambled all of these body riddles! Write the letter of the correct answer beside each question.

_____ 1. What do you call a corpulent kitty?

_____ 2. Why were the worms in Appletree County so happy?

_____ 3. How is a baker like a corsage-maker?

_____ 4. Who wrote the book *Is Life Over When The Carnival Ends*?

_____ 5. What company specializes in practical jokes and magic tricks?

_____ 6. Who wrote the book *Carnage In The Forest*?

_____ 7. What is the official flower of the city of Detroit?

_____ 8. What is another name for a red lizard?

_____ 9. What do you call a corpse with chicken pox?

_____ 10. What kind of carnivore lived in the West millions of years ago?

_____ 11. For which Laff-Olympic event do you wear a corset?

_____ 12. What kind of dance do mosquitoes like to do?

a. Trouble Incorporated

b. Midas Welby

c. The girdle hurdle

d. A spotty body

e. Tim Burr

f. A carnelian chameleon

g. Tyrannosaurus Tex

h. They both have their hands full of flower.

i. They had esprit de core.

j. A fat cat

k. The Corpuscle Hustle

l. The car-nation

WORKING WITH
-CARN-
-CORP-
WORDS

It's time to go shopping! Help Rootster find what he needs. For each question below, write the letter of the best answer.

Where should Rootster go if . . .

_____ 1. he needs a corset?
_____ 2. he needs corpuscles?
_____ 3. he is a carnivore?
_____ 4. he wants to investigate reincarnation?
_____ 5. he needs a corsage for a dance?
_____ 6. he wants a carnelian?
_____ 7. he likes growing carnations?
_____ 8. he needs to incorporate?
_____ 9. he hates hearing about carnage?
_____ 10. he is corpulent?
_____ 11. he is a corporal?
_____ 12. he plans to attend a carnival?
_____ 13. he needs to take care of a corpse?
_____ 14. he wants to improve his esprit de corps?

WORDTOWN, U.S.A.

a. Patsy's Prom Posies
b. Red Meat Cafe
c. Good News Boutique
d. Myrtle's Girdles & Lingerie
e. Tiny Tim's Diet Center
f. Ozzie's Costumes & Disguises
g. Miss Keet O'Byte's Blood Bank
h. Bobby Snatcher's Funeral Home
i. The Soldiers' Commissary
j. Back-To-Life Bookstore
k. Ruby's Gems & Jewels
l. The Cheerleaders' Pep Shop
m. Red's Bud & Bulb Shop
n. The Legal Eagle, specializing in group and organization law

-PED-, -POD- foot

biped	*pedestal*	*pedometer*
centipede	*pedestrian*	*podiatrist*
decapod	*pediatric*	*podiatry*
impediment	*pediatrician*	*podium*
pedagogue	*pedicure*	*quadruped*
pedal	*pedigree*	*tripod*

Unit Kickoff

Place a nail file, a little plastic crab, a toy soldier and a *pedometer* in a small paper bag. Ask for volunteers to feel inside the bag and guess its contents without looking. After several tries, show the items and supply these words with a common root: *pedicure, decapod, biped*, and *pedometer*. Explain that all the words in this unit will share the idea of foot in their meaning.

Word Exploration Ideas

Do any students have pets with *pedigrees?* Invite them to explain the process of registering an animal with a breeder's association. (The connection between this word and foot is a visual one; the ancient Romans thought an ancestry chart looked like a crane's foot!)

Pass out *pedometers* and have students meaure distances to various locations at your school.

Challenge future physicians to decide whether the following problems would be treated by a *pediatrician* or a *podiatrist:* chicken pox, corns and calluses, allergies, flu, bunions, bursitis, fever, runny nose, shin splints, ingrown toenails, earache.

What are some safety rules regarding *pedestrians*? Divide students into teams to write and record musical jingles that could help young children learn these rules.

Post student-written reports of important *pedagogues* on a bulletin board. Students may research any of the following: Maria Montessori, Jean Piaget, Plato, Socrates, Louis Braille, Mary McLeod Bethune, John Dewey, Horace Mann, William H. McGuffey, B. F. Skinner, Booker T. Washington, Noah Webster. (Another interesting note: the word *pedagogue* originally meant the servant who led the student to school.)

Combine this root with number prefixes for some fun with feet! With *biped* and *quadruped* as examples, brainstorm with students what the scientific terms might be for animals of one, three, five, six, seven, eight, or nine legs.

READING FOR MEANING
-PED-, -POD-
foot

This certainly is a change of scene, Rootster!

After a farewell feast of spicy Cajun **decapods**, Rootster whisks us north to Cambridge, Massachusetts. We land at Harvard University, an institution with an impressive **pedigree**. We see a large statue on a **pedestal** in the main building on campus. **Pedagogues** have labored at this university since its founding in 1636. Through the decades, they have stood at **podiums** in lecture halls, imparting knowledge to undergraduate and graduate students.

We watch as **pedestrians** and **pedal**-pushers rush to class, possibly to study animal life of all kinds— **bipeds**, **quadrupeds**, even **centipedes**. Medical students may be dreaming of a career in **pediatrics**, **podiatry**, or another specialty. Young artists paint. Writers write. Photographers set up their **tripods**.

Some students think that excessive noise is an **impediment** to learning. Someone has posted a sign, *Quiet: Great Minds At Work!*, near the entrance to one of the buildings.

ROOTING FOR MEANING
-PED-, -POD-

Write definitions for the boldfaced words. Refer to a dictionary. Include the root meaning (foot) in each definition.
Example: pedestrian—a person who travels on foot

ROOTSTER'S -PED-, -POD- RIDDLES

The answers to some of Rootster's wacky vocabulary riddles are listed below. Write the number of the matching question beside each one.

_____ A. Stan Wellback.

_____ B. Kiddie City.

_____ C. "Hey, man, you're way off-base!"

_____ D. A tripod squad.

_____ E. Earl E. Mann.

_____ F. A red quadruped.

_____ G. There is no time to play after they get their golf shoes on!

_____ H. A pedal medal.

_____ I. Jay Walker.

_____ J. Xavier Breth.

_____ K. A flea with a pedigree.

_____ L. A creature teacher.

_____ M. Footstools.

_____ N. Because he sells stop-sicles!

1. What has four feet and blushes at corny jokes?

2. What do you call a Martian pedagogue?

3. Why is the ice cream man such an impediment to traffic?

4. Who wrote the book *How to Study Decapods*?

5. What kind of mushrooms do podiatrists like?

6. A statue at the art museum slipped off its pedestal. What did the other statues say?

7. Who wrote the book *The First Bipeds*?

8. What do you call the pediatric ward of a hospital?

9. How come centipedes don't play golf?

10. What do you call a team of photographers?

11. Who wrote the book *Rules for Pedestrians*?

12. What do you call the baby bug whose ancestors bit Washington's horse, Lincoln's cat, and Roosevelt's rabbit?

13. Who wrote the book *Boring Speeches at the Podium*?

14. What do you give the winner of a bike race?

WORKING WITH
-PED-, -POD-
WORDS

Welcome to Rootster's Hall of Fame! For each question below, fill in the letter of the correct answer.

_____ 1. Who had a stuffed *quadruped* named in his honor?

_____ 2. Who wrote about *decapods* and other sea life in her ecology books?

_____ 3. Who gave the United States a lady on a *pedestal?*

_____ 4. Who overcame the *impediment* of polio to serve four terms as President?

_____ 5. What *pedestrian* planted apple trees throughout the American wilderness?

_____ 6. Who gave a famous speech at Gettysburg, Pennsylvania—possibly from a *podium?*

_____ 7. Who invented the first *pedal*-powered sewing machine?

_____ 8. Who was Helen Keller's *pedagogue?*

_____ 9. Who probably encountered *centipedes* as he guided John Fremont to California?

_____ 10. Who was the first *biped* to set foot on the moon?

_____ 11. What *pediatrician* wrote a best-selling guide to child care?

_____ 12. Who developed a camera that people could use without a *tripod?*

_____ 13. Who made a fortune marketing *podiatric* products?

_____ 14. What statesman did not like to place importance on a person's *pedigree?*

a. Franklin D. Roosevelt

b. Dr. William Scholl

c. Kit Carson

d. France

e. George Eastman

f. Isaac M. Singer

g. Thomas Jefferson

h. John Chapman (Johnny Appleseed)

i. Rachel Carson

j. Annie Sullivan

k. Teddy Roosevelt

l. Dr. Benjamin Spock

m. Abraham Lincoln

n. Neil Armstrong

-MANU- hand

emancipate	*maneuver*	*manual*
manacle	*manicure*	*manufacture*
manage	*manifest*	*manure*
mandate	*manipulate*	
mandatory	*manner*	

Unit Kickoff

Tell the students that during the mid-1800s, some people felt that the expansion of the United States was inevitable, and that the government would one day govern all of North America. This concept was known as **Manifest** Destiny. As a result of this concept, the United States made many territorial acquisitions that are now part of the country.

Follow up the discussion of Manifest Destiny with an analysis of the word's literal Latin meaning: *manu* (hand) and *festus* (hit, hit by the hand, obvious, readily apparent). Ask students to list other words that are formed from the root -MANU-.

Word Exploration Ideas

Table **manners** involve how people behave when they eat. Students will find the history of manners fascinating. Have students check out library books on manners and etiquette from different periods of history. Hold a class discussion on how manners have changed over time and from place to place.

Two words on this list can be applied to the era of slavery in America, **manacle** and **emancipation**. If possible, play a recording of African-American spirituals (such as "Go Down, Moses") for your students. Have the students listen for lyrics that evoke the meanings of these two unit words.

Scholars believe the game of chess began as an exercise in military **maneuvers**. Set up a chess board and have students who know how to play demonstrate some strategies for their classmates.

The practice of **manicuring** and painting one's fingernails has been around for thousands of years. Hypothesize with students the social and cultural significance of groomed nails.

READING FOR MEANING
-MANU-
hand

Rootster, where are we going now?

Our energetic pilot **maneuvers** in his seat to toss something to us. It is a pair of pants. We examine them. From the **manner** in which they are constructed, we realize the pants were not **manufactured**, but rather, sewn **manually**.

"Those are bloomers," Rootster tells us. "And in the 1850s, they **emancipated** women from the **manacles** of clumsy clothing. We are on the way to Seneca Falls, New York, where bloomers became **mandatory** dress for early women's rights activists."

Elizabeth Smith Miller discovered bloomers while on her honeymoon in Europe. In them she was able to **manage** hiking in the Swiss mountains. After she returned, she met Angela Jenks Bloomer who also preferred the new style of dress to the uncomfortable dresses **mandated** by social etiquette. An article in Mrs. Bloomer's feminist paper, *The Lily*, soon convinced many that bloomers were the **manifest** attire for comfort and practicality.

ROOTING FOR MEANING
-MANU-

Write definitions for the boldfaced words. Refer to a dictionary. Include a root meaning (hand) in each definition.
Example: manipulate—to operate with the hands, to handle to one's own advantage.

Name _____

ROOTSTER'S -MANU- RIDDLES

Rootster is filling in today for the town librarian. For each book title below, write the letter of the correct author.

_____ 1. *The Complete Guide to Manicures*	a. by Otto Moe Beal
_____ 2. *Mandate for Marriage*	b. by Claire S. Mudd
_____ 3. *The Little Kid's Book of Good Manners*	c. by Ella Funt Trayner
_____ 4. *Lincoln, the Emancipator*	d. by Ono I. Brokanale
_____ 5. *The Future in Manufacturing*	e. by Todd Lerr
_____ 6. *Mandatory Requirements for Drivers*	f. by Frea Last
_____ 7. *50 Tricky Maneuvers for Magicians*	g. by Al B. Wedd
_____ 8. *The Vegetable Manual*	h. by Dee Kee
_____ 9. *Managing Big Animals*	i. by L. Bow
_____ 10. *Manure for Great Gardens*	j. by Howie Did It
_____ 11. *No Longer Manifest*	k. by Brock O. Lee
_____ 12. *How to Unlock Any Manacle*	l. by Hans Doolittle
_____ 13. *Manipulating Macaroni*	m. by Ida Hoe and Ken Hardlee Standit

Now, Rootster has to recommend the best book for each person below. Using the titles above, write in the number of the correct choice.

What is the best book for . .

_____ A. A chef who handles a lot of sticky pasta?

_____ B. A criminal frequently placed in handcuffs?

_____ C. A king outlawing bachelorhood?

_____ D. A scientist designing robots for assembly-line work?

_____ E. Cinderella's dishpan hands?

_____ F. A circus owner?

_____ G. A farmer trying to sell cows' organic waste?

_____ H. A teenager needing to know license laws?

_____ I. An imprisoned slave?

_____ J. An illusionist who is all thumbs?

_____ K. A child who eats with his fingers?

_____ L. A housewife who wants to cook a new side dish?

_____ M. A politician who needs to cover up an obvious problem?

WORKING WITH -MANU- WORDS

emancipate	maneuver	manual
manacle	manicure	manufacture
manage	manifest	manure
mandate	manipulate	
mandatory	manner	

Oh-oh! Rootster has found some more mixed-up sentences. Can you right these wrongs? Cross out each vocabulary word used incorrectly. Write the correct word on the line.

1. The woman spent hours with files and creams, manacling her nails. _____

2. To test some new equipment, the Marines conducted manures at a desert military base. _____

3. "Manifest me! Manifest me!" the pirate's prisoner cried. _____

4. "This landslide victory is a maneuver by the people!" the politician told the crowd. "While in office, I promise to carry out your orders!" _____

5. Almost everyone enjoys five-year olds, but not everyone knows how to manufacture a classroom full of them! _____

6. The manuals were so tight, they left sores on the suspect's wrists. _____

7. The celebrity's down-to-earth manicure put all of us at ease. _____

8. A good friend does not emancipate you to do things that you should not do. _____

9. This mandate should improve the soil in my garden, but shoveling it is less than pleasant. _____

10. The need for improved study habits was manipulated by his poor report card. _____

11. Pre-registration for the conference is mannerly. No walk-ins will be permitted. _____

12. When in doubt, consult the service mandatory. _____

13. Thomas Edison developed a process to successfully manage the light bulb. _____

-ARCH- first, leader

anarchy
archangel
archaeology
archaeopteryx
archaic

archetype
archipelago
architect
archive

hierarchy
matriarch
monarch
oligarchy

Unit Kickoff

Provide reference materials for prehistoric animals. Ask students to look up the names of animals that begin with the root -ARCH-. What idea do all the names share? Explain that the root can mean first in time, or first in importance. Some examples are listed below:

Archaeopteryx (Ancient Wing)
Archaeornithomimus (Ancient Bird Mimic)
Archelon (Ruler Tortoise)

All the words on the list for this unit are *first* words, as in early, beginning, ruling, or leading.

Word Exploration Ideas

Continue your prehistoric animal theme with some imaginative artwork and creative thinking. What kinds of dinosaur names can students dream up by combining some of the word roots they have studied? What would an archaeopedasaur look like? How about a carniportus? Have students draw the dinosaurs that they create and explain their unique features.

Display photos of buildings by famous **architects** such as Frank Lloyd Wright, I. M. Pei, Filippo Brunelleschi, Andrea Palladio, Sir Christopher Wren, Mies van der Rohe, and Le Corbusier. Challenge students to draw their own dream houses.

Challenge each student to draw an **archetype** of a vehicle that might be used 50 years in the future. Have the students explain the advantages of their vehicles to a partner.

Conduct an **archipelago** hunt on a world map. Some well-known archipelagos are the Aegean Islands off the coast of Greece, the Lofoten Islands off the coast of Norway, and the Malay Archipelago between southeast Asia and Australia .

READING FOR MEANING
-ARCH-
first, leader

> Ah-choo! Where is this dust coming from, Rootster?

> We're visiting a museum today, my friends. Within the rooms of this **architectural** dinosaur, we will see many **archaic** but fascinating objects and displays.

"There is something for everyone here!" exclaims our pilot. "Located in the **Archives** Department are historical documents that saved our young nation from **anarchy**. In another area are **architectural** blueprints of major cities, as well as primitive maps of newly discovered **archipelagos**. And for you **archaeology** nuts, there are artifacts and relics from ancient cultures.

"But that's not all," Rootster continues. "The walls in one wing are covered with art. Here is a drawing of an **archangel** and a portrait of a Mexican **monarch**. Another painting depicts a large tribe of natives gathered around its **matriarch**.

"This museum collects the best of the old. It is managed by an **oligarchy** of experts." Our tour guide looks thoughtful. "I wonder if there are any job openings here. I'd like to work my way up the **hierarchy**. Just imagine your old friend, Rootster, as director of this museum. . ."

Before he gets lost in his dreams, we grab the Rootster and run for the plane!

ROOTING FOR MEANING
-ARCH-

Write definitions for the boldfaced words. Refer to a dictionary. Include the root meaning (first or leader) in each definition.
Example: architect—lead or master builder

ROOTSTER'S -ARCH- RIDDLES

Read the vocabulary riddles below. Write the letter of the matching answer in each blank.

_____ 1. What do you call a nation led by a few dogs?

_____ 2. What machine do archaeologists use most?

_____ 3. Foreign visitors always brought jewels for a particular monarch's fingers. Why?

_____ 4. What do you call your mother's favorite playground?

_____ 5. What happened to the archaeopteryx who crashed into a tyrannosaurus rex?

_____ 6. What kind of house plans do ghostly architects draw?

_____ 7. The scribe watched the anarchy around him, carefully writing down everything that happened. Why?

_____ 8. What is the one thing archangels won't eat?

_____ 9. What do you call a TV show about archives?

_____ 10. What do you call a friendly archipelago?

_____ 11. A man applied for a job. First he had to talk to one boss, then another, then still another. Why?

_____ 12. What do you call the archetype for a fancy new canteen?

_____ 13. What do you call archaic treasure?

a. She got a dino-sore.

b. Isles of Smiles.

c. Because he was a king with a thing for a ring

d. Boo-prints.

e. Old gold.

f. A barky oligarchy.

g. Devil's food cake.

h. Because he was the disorder recorder.

i. Because it was the hire-archy.

j. A bottle model.

k. The arti-fax.

l. Matriarch Park.

m. A document-ary.

WORKING WITH
-ARCH-
WORDS

Who said that? For each quotation below, write the letter of the speaker who might have said it.

_____ 1. "Listen, young whippersnapper! Shape up and fly right, or I'll have to take your halo away!"

_____ 2. "I only make small decisions. I pass the bigger ones on to the next official. Then he passes the most important decisions on to our leader."

_____ 3. "As a kid I designed treehouses and play forts. Now I design high-rise office buildings."

_____ 4. "Bones, bones, bones. All I ever see is crummy old bones!"

_____ 5. "Excuse me, but I must have taken the wrong flight pattern. Can someone kindly direct me to the Jurassic Period?"

_____ 6. "I was the first. All the others are just copies of me. Who was the original? Moi!"

_____ 7. "As a kid, he caused trouble in school. Now he causes trouble for the government!"

_____ 8. "Oh, dear, where did I file that old record book. It's got to be here somewhere!"

_____ 9. "I'll summon all the women so we can decide the future of our country."

_____ 10. "My queen and I shall dine with the Knights of the Round Table this evening. Inform the Royal Chef to prepare my favorite dish, Four-and-Twenty-Blackbirds, baked in a pie."

_____ 11. "Listen, those dumb club members don't know what to do. The three of us will make all the decisions, okay?"

_____ 12. "Land-Ho! I see hundreds of tiny islands, like jewels on a necklace!"

_____ 13. "This old thing? Why, I've had it for years and years and years. Yes, it's very out-of-date, but I still value it."

   a. A matriarch
   b. An archive-keeper
   c. A monarch
   d. An anarchist
   e. An archaeopteryx
   f. An archetype
   g. The owner of an archaic object
   h. An architect
   i. An archaeologist
   j. An archangel
   k. An explorer discovering an archipelago
   l. A member of a hierarchy
   m. The leader of an oligarchy

-PRIMO-, -PROTO- first

prima donna	*prince*
primary	*principal*
primate	*principle*
primer	*protagonist*
primeval	*protein*
primitive	*protocol*
primogenitor	*protoplasm*

Unit Kickoff

Introduce these "first" words with student dramatizations
of the following situations:
• a ***prima donna*** observing ***protoplasm*** through a microscope
• a ***primate*** attempting to read a ***primer***
• a ***prince*** bungling ***protocol***
Divide the class into small groups and allow a few minutes for
looking up the words and planning the skits. As each group
performs, the rest of the class attempts to identify the correct
vocabulary words from a list on the board. Point out the idea
common to all the featured words, the root meaning, first.

Word Exploration Ideas

The word ***prima donna*** comes to us from the world of the opera. Introduce your students to this
fascinating art form with a taste of one of the lighter operas, such as *The Magic Flute* by Mozart or
the American classic, *Porgy and Bess* by George Gershwin. Create a supplementary vocabulary list
with opera terms such as overture, aria, score, libretto, interlude, repertoire.

"This is the forest ***primeval***. The murmuring pines and the hemlocks . . . stand like Druids of
old . . ." These famous lines open Henry Wadsworth Longfellow's narrative poem, *Evangeline*, the
tragic tale of two lovers separated by war and politics, who remain faithful to the end. Read the
poem with your students.

Discuss the difference between ***protocol*** and manners. What situations call for simple good manners
and which dictate a more formalized code of behavior?

Challenge your students to write a melodramatic play using some of the unit words. Help them get
started by setting up a plot with the following elements:

Setting: a primeval forest	Villain: a wild primate
Protagonist: a prince	Victim: a prima donna

READING FOR MEANING
-PRIMO-, -PROTO-
first

*Get out your **protocol primers**, Vocab-Travelers! We're going to visit the **prince** who lives in that **primeval** castle down there.*

We land in one of the smallest countries in the world. Its many tourist attractions are a ***primary*** source of revenue. An excellent museum displays ***primitive*** tools used by the nation's first inhabitants. A zoo includes a large collection of ***primates*** from all over the globe. Here also is a research center where ***protoplasm, proteins*** and other life-giving elements have been studied since the early 1900's. The luxury hotels that dot the coast treat every guest like a pampered ***prima donna***.

We long to stretch out on the beach, but Rootster reminds us of our appointment with the Prince, the ***protagonist*** in this country's success story. This dignified ruler shares his ***principal*** concern with us. He needs to make the most of every inch of this postage-stamp country. "And who will be the next ruler?" someone asks. "According to our ***principle*** of ***primogeniture***, my oldest son will be the next head of state," the Prince explains.

Our group sighs. Some kids have all the luck!

ROOTING FOR MEANING
-PRIMO-, -PROTO-

Write definitions for the boldfaced words. Refer to a dictionary. Include the root meaning (first) in each definition.

Example: primitive—in the first stages of development

ROOTSTER'S -PRIMO-, -PROTO- RIDDLES

Not again! Someone has scrambled all of Rootster's "first" riddles! Write the letter of the correct answer beside each question.

_____ 1. What's a protagonist's favorite snack?

_____ 2. What did the mother vampire tell her son before he left for the school dance?

_____ 3. What do you call an ancient bug with a taste for plants?

_____ 4. Which ship do principals admire most?

_____ 5. What did the caveman say to compliment his girlfriend?

_____ 6. With whom should you talk if you want to learn more about primogenitors?

_____ 7. According to White House protocol, what happens if the Secret Service agent forgets the President's umbrella?

_____ 8. What keeps protoplasm together?

_____ 9. What did the big primate say to the little primate?

_____ 10. What kind of textbook do beginning readers prefer?

_____ 11. How can you tell if a prima donna is going bald?

_____ 12. When the president of a large candy company had a new baby boy, what did folks call the little fellow?

_____ 13. The caveman noticed that when he held a certain stone near another stone, the two clicked together and were difficult to separate. What had the caveman discovered?

_____ 14. What do you call a beginner in Tinkerbelle's School of Enchantment?

    a. Cell-ophane tape

    b. "You're so primitive, dear!"

    c. A primary fairy

    d. He gets wet.

    e. "Don't monkey with me, son!"

    f. A hero sandwich

    g. Scholarship

    h. The Prince of Mints

    i. "Make sure you get plenty of pro-teens tonight, dear!"

    j. A primeval weevil

    k. Your aunt's sisters (ancestors)

    l. A trimmer primer

    m. See if she puts on any (h)airs.

    n. The Princi-pulls of Magnetism

WORKING WITH
-PRIMO-,
-PROTO-
WORDS

prima donna	primitive	protagonist
primary	primogenitor	protein
primate	prince	protocol
primer	principal	protoplasm
primeval	principle	

Remember Rootster's motto, K.I.S.S.! Re-write each wordy sentence below in eight words or less. Use words from the word box.

1. The lead female singer, who was very vain and sensitive, voiced many loud demands for her own room in which to change her costume.

2. A researcher in natural phenomena from Germany studied and named the matter that comprises a living cell in 1839.

3. No matter what awaits me, I am determined that I will not give up my personal beliefs simply to ensure that I have plenty of friends.

4. It would be extremely wise to make sure that you understand the etiquette and customs of a person's country before you make a social call.

5. Doctors who treat childhood illnesses and diseases have learned that in many cases the very youngest children of all seem to get a great deal of pleasure from the three most basic colors, the ones that cannot be made by mixing other colors together.

6. The main character and hero featured in the novel struggled with an enormous number of very difficult problems to come out on top.

7. The race of people who come from the tiny Mediterranean country bordered by Arab nations trace their ancestry back to a man named Abraham.

8. The men who worked at imparting knowledge did their utmost with great energy to make sure the monarch's son was ready to assume his royal duties.

9. The decorative patterns scratched onto the side of the molded earthen receptacle were of the earliest stage of cultural development.

10. Jane Goodall has devoted a lifetime to the careful examination of the man-like mammals that live on the African continent.

11. The books that were first printed in this country for the purpose of teaching children how to read presented the alphabet in poetic verse.

12. It is imperative that we keep in an unchanged state the extremely old wooded regions that continue to exist.

13. Consume foods that contain the essential chemicals in order to help your body form a strong skeletal system and the supporting tissues that expand and contract.

-MATER-, -PATER- mother, father

alma mater	*matron*	*patriot*
maternity	*paternity*	*patronize*
matriculate	*patriarch*	*patronym*
matrimony	*patrician*	*pattern*

Unit Kickoff

Discuss wedding traditions such as serving cake, throwing rice, and tying old shoes to the newlyweds' car. According to its roots, the unit word ***matrimony*** literally means the formal act of entering into motherhood. The custom of throwing rice began as a fertility rite to wish a couple the blessing of many children. Your students will enjoy researching the historical background of other matrimonial customs and elements such as the ring, the best man, the veil, and the white dress.

Word Exploration Ideas

What do the surnames Johnson, Jones, Jensen, Johanson, Janowicz, Ivanov, Janosfi, and MacEoin have in common? They are all ***patronyms***, meaning *son of John* in various languages. Provide name books and encourage students to look up the origin and meaning of common names.

A sage once observed that there are no requirements for two of the hardest jobs on earth: ***maternity*** and ***paternity***. With your class, write a job description for each position. It's interesting to see what qualities students identify as most important!

Give interested students a list of biblical men (Moses, Daniel, Abraham, Isaiah, Jacob, Samuel, Isaac, Cain, Samson, Jonah) and ask them to decide which ones were the ***patriarchs*** of the Israelites. Exodus 3:16 provides the answer (Abraham, Isaac, and Jacob).

Who coined the terms *summer soldier* and *sunshine **patriot***? Show students how to locate famous sayings in Bartlett's *Familiar Quotations* or a similar reference. (Thomas Paine, the essayist of the American Revolution, used the terms to describe those who favored independence as long as it was easily secured.)

Point out that in Roman times, the opposite of a wealthy ***patrician*** was a plebeian, one of the common people. Just for fun, have the students write cheers for the Pats and the Plebs.

READING FOR MEANING

-MATER-, -PATER-
mother, father

On an eastern flight **pattern**, we land near a beautiful campus. "My **alma mater**," Rootster explains. "I **matriculated** here when I was just a boy."

A pleasant young **matron** helps an elderly **patriarch** out to our plane. Rootster runs to meet them. "Dr. Nobles! Susan! How are you? Where's Paul?"

The woman laughs and straightens her **maternity** dress. "We're just fine, as you can see, Rootster. Paul is away on a government assignment. He is quite the **patriot**, you know. Father and I are running the school while he is gone."

Rootster gives the woman a **patronizing** pat on the shoulder. "Paul's **paternal** instincts will bring him home soon. Have you decided what to name Junior?"

Susan laughs. "Rootster, how did you guess? Yes, we're going to use a **patronym**: Paul, Jr. if it's a boy and Paula if it's a girl. I'm sure our baby will have Paul's **patrician** features."

Hours later, after we have toured the campus and visited with Rootster's friends, we pile back in the plane. "What a relaxing stop," Rootster sighs. "Perhaps I'll settle down some day and consider **matrimony**."

ROOTING FOR MEANING
-MATER-, -PATER-

Write definitions for the boldfaced words. Refer to a dictionary. Include a root meaning (mother or father) in each definition.
Example: patrician—coming from the class of founding fathers; aristocratic

ROOTSTER'S -MATER-, -PATER- RIDDLES

The answers to some more of Rootster's vocabulary riddles are listed below. Write the number of the matching question beside each one.

_____ A. A llama mama
_____ B. Orlando D. Free and Homer D. Brave
_____ C. A fat aristocrat
_____ D. George Washington, the "father of our country"
_____ E. "Wanna trace?"
_____ F. The Patri-Ark
_____ G. To a nursery school
_____ H. A restaurant, because the owners are always at lunch
_____ I. "Your patronym!"
_____ J. The school of hard knocks
_____ K. Great Expectations
_____ L. Phony matrimony

1. What would Noah have called his boat if he had put grandfathers on it instead of animals?
2. What do you call a pretend wedding?
3. What do you call an overfed patrician?
4. What did the pencil say to the pattern?
5. What do you call a matronly South American animal?
6. What was the name of the stuntman's alma mater?
7. Which American is famous for his paternity?
8. Which patriots are mentioned in our national anthem?
9. What's a good name for a store that sells maternity clothing?
10. When Mrs. Oak's seedlings were old enough to matriculate, where did she send them?
11. What business is very hard to patronize?
12. "Jim, Jr.," Big Jim asked, "What belongs to you that came from me, but is used more by everyone else?"
    "Gee, Dad," Jim Jr. said, "I give up. What?"

WORKING WITH
-MATER-, -PATER-
WORDS

Do you remember K.I.S.S., where you shrink wordy sentences down into short ones? Now Rootster wants you to do the opposite! Take each short sentence below and make it as long and wordy as you can. See if you can use 20 or more words in each sentence. Refer to a dictionary.

Example: The French Riviera is a patrician's playground.
The southern section of France that borders on the Mediterranean Sea is the spot where a wealthy upper-class individual can go to relax and have fun.

1. Matrons dread their children's matriculations.

2. Businesswomen do not want to be patronized.

3. Matrimony is a most serious undertaking.

4. The patrician patronized his alma mater.

5. Some children do not appreciate their patronyms.

6. Maternity seems to last an eternity.

7. Matricide is a crime society abhors.

8. A true patriot sacrifices self to serve.

9. The patriarch models a positive pattern of behavior for his family.

-SPEC-, -SPIC- to look

circumspect	*retrospective*	*spectrum*
expect	*species*	*speculate*
inconspicuous	*spectacle*	*suspicious*
inspector	*spectator*	
introspective	*specter*	

Unit Kickoff

Dim the lights in your classroom and tell your students a story of a *specter* to create interest in words that relate to any visual appearance, spooky or otherwise! Instruct students in the use of etymological dictionary listings to come up with as many words as possible that share the -SPEC-/-SPIC- root. Additional words are auspicious, perspective, perspicacity, prospectus, special, specific, specimen, specious, and speculum.

Word Exploration Ideas

Celebrate the color *spectrum* with Rainbow Day. Enlist students' help in collecting art work, objects, literature, mythology, songs and scientific information about the seven bands of light we call the rainbow.

How many different *species* of animals and insects exist in the world today? No one knows for sure, but scientists *speculate* there are more than two million. Invite a veterinarian or other animal expert to class to present basic information about animal classification.

Assign independent research on the development of *spectacles*, or have students survey several classrooms to determine the number of students who wear glasses. Have students graph the results of their survey and then project an estimate of the number for the entire school.

Plan with students effective ways to create personal *retrospective* histories—through journals, scrapbooks, time capsules, autobiographies, or graphs of personal ups and downs.

Your students will enjoy discussing the personality differences between an *instropective* individual and an extrovert. As a class, list traits of each and analyze their best and worst features. When do students appreciate an extrovert? When is *introspection* a valuable asset? Have students classify themselves and think about which personality type they seek in friendships.

READING FOR MEANING
-SPEC-, -SPIC-
look

Rootster, look! It's a rainbow!

We watch in wonder as our plane emerges from the clouds to pass through a **spectrum** of sunlight. It's quite a **spectacle!** Soon Rootster lands beside a field of fragrant bushes. We sniff the air and **speculate** about the source of the scent. "Tea—the air smells like tea!" someone cries.

In a shed nearby, **inspectors** are sorting leaves. Although there are many different teas available, most of them are made from one **species** of plant.

The tea pickers watch us **suspiciously** until Rootster convinces them that we mean no harm. Then they invite us to a traditional tea ceremony. We settle into an **inconspicuous** corner. As **spectators**, we are not sure just what to **expect**. The tea master prepares the tea and hands a small, steaming cup to Rootster. He sips **circumspectly**. "Hmmm," says our **introspective** pilot. "Interesting flavor."

That night we discuss the events of the day. "In **retrospect**, it was tea-rific!" a passenger jokes.

ROOTING FOR MEANING
-SPEC-, -SPIC-

Write definitions for the boldfaced words. Refer to a dictionary. Include the root meaning (look) in each definition.
Example: introspective—the characteristic of looking inward, to one's self

ROOTSTER'S -SPEC-, -SPIC- RIDDLES

These questions and answers are matched up correctly, but someone has left out the most important words! Fill in each blank with a vocabulary word from this unit.

1. What instrument lets you _____ monsters?
   A horro-scope.

2. What _____ of insects are the most nervous?
   Jitterbugs.

3. What did the _____ little pebble say?
   "I wish I were a little boulder (bolder)."

4. What man _____ to shave more than ten times a day?
   A barber.

5. What goes through water but doesn't get wet?
   A _____ of light.

6. What did the old vampire artist say at the _____ held in his honor?
   "Fangs for the memory!"

7. Why was the man _____ of what the sardine said?
   It sounded too fishy.

8. What do you have to know to _____ in real estate?
   Lots.

9. Who make the best _____ at jousting tournaments?
   Knight watchmen.

10. What did the reading glasses say to the sunshades?
    "Don't make such a _____ of yourself!"

11. Why do you want to be _____ in cannibal territory?
    You don't want to get into a stew!

12. Why is copper an _____ metal?
    Because it is all in the mine (mind).

13. What did the girl _____ say to the boy _____?
    "You don't stand a ghost of a chance with me!"

| circumspect |
| expect |
| inconspicuous |
| inspect |
| introspective |
| retrospective |
| species |
| spectacle |
| spectator |
| specter |
| spectrum |
| speculate |
| suspicious |

WORKING WITH -SPEC-, -SPIC- WORDS

circumspect	retrospect	spectrum
expect	species	speculate
inconspicuous	spectacle	suspicious
inspect	spectator	
introspection	specter	

When Rootster tells a fairy tale, he uses plenty of great vocabulary words.
Fill in the missing words from this Rootster-tale.

Once upon a word, a little girl sat on a stump, lost in (1)_____. As she thought, she
stared at a (2)_____ of light that arched through the forest. Just then, her mother
called, with an errand for the little girl to run.

"Take this basket to Grandma," the mother said. "Watch out for dangerous (3)_____ in
the woods. Be (4)_____ about the people you meet." The little girl's mother
squinted at the sun. "You should be home by dark," she (5)_____.

So the little girl started down the path to her grandmother's house. She did not know she had a
(6)_____ as she skipped through the woods. She did not realize that her picnic
basket was very (7)_____.

When her grandmother did not answer the door, the little girl grew very (8)_____.
She went inside and (9)_____ the creature lying in bed. "Gracious!" the little girl
cried. "I must need new (10) _____, or else you have grown extremely ugly,
Grandma!"

"What did you (11)_____?" snapped the creature in bed, "A beauty queen?"

The little girl acted as if she had seen a (12)_____. She grabbed her basket and ran
all the way home.

In (13)_____, her mother said, "I should not have sent you to Grandma's house by
yourself."

Now it's your turn! See if you can tell a fairy tale
in Rootster's style. Try to use all the words from
this vocabulary unit. Suggested stories are *The
Three Little Pigs, Goldilocks and the Three Bears,*
and *Jack and the Beanstalk.*

-MONO-, -UNI- one

monarch

monastery

monk

monocle

monogamy

monologue

monopoly

monotone

uniform

union

unique

unison

universe

Unit Kickoff

Should students be required to wear **uniforms** to school? Is a **unique** outfit a healthy form of self-expression? Should Congress adopt a **universal** dress code for students throughout the entire **Union**? Interest students in this list of words with a debate on student dress. You can be sure the discussion will not be **monotonous**!

Word Exploration Ideas

Conduct a school **uniform** design contest. Set some guidelines for your budding fashion designers. The school outfit must be appropriate for all shapes and sizes of students. It must be affordable and readily available. It must be comfortable for normal school activities. Post the contestants' design sketches and vote for the most popular design.

One of the most popular board games of all time takes its name from a word in this unit, **monopoly**. Challenge students to create their own version of this game, using locations in and around your school as game board squares.

Each human being possesses a combination of characteristics that make him or her **unique**. Direct students in this thinking exercise. Have each student write the letters of his or her first name vertically. Beside each letter, the student writes a personal trait beginning with the same letter. Have a thesaurus and dictionaries available. The finished products will reveal one-of-a-kind students!

Select a narrative poem suitable for choral reading. With the students, decide which sections should be read in **unison**, and which would be better spoken as **monologues**. Have the students practice the reading before they present it.

READING FOR MEANING
-MONO-, -UNI-
one

"Monkeys!" the passengers cry in **unison**. "That's correct," Rootster replies. "We're at a **monastery** in the Asian country of Nepal. The Buddhist **monks** here feed the wild monkeys and let them climb on the temple roof."

Rootster clears his throat and begins a long **monologue** in a **monotone** voice. We don't stay to listen, but hop off the plane to learn about the monkeys firsthand. Everywhere we turn, we see the lively mammals—all shapes and sizes. It's a virtual monkey **universe**!

One monkey stares at us. His reddish fur reminds us of a **uniform**, and he sports a handsome white mustache. "If this guy had a **monocle**, he would look like a real **monarch**!" a passenger laughs.

Over our heads, two gibbons care for their baby. "When a pair of gibbons forms a **union**, it is for life. They are **monogamous**, you know," a monk tells us. He points to a pile of coconuts under a tree. "Thanks to our monkey workers, our **monastery** has a **monopoly** on the coconut trade in town. The monkeys pick the coconuts for us and we pay them in bananas!"

Much too soon, it is time to board the plane. Of all the places Rootster has taken us, this corner of Nepal is certainly **unique**.

ROOTING FOR MEANING
-MONO-, -UNI-

Write definitions for the boldfaced words. Refer to a dictionary. Include the root meaning (one) in each definition.

Example: monologue—words spoken by one person

ROOTSTER'S -MONO-, -UNI- RIDDLES

Read the vocabulary riddles below. Write the letter of the matching answer in each blank.

_____ 1. Who wrote the book *My Fast-Food Monopoly?*
_____ 2. Where did the monarch go for entertainment?
_____ 3. What did the fireman say when the monastery caught fire?
_____ 4. What happened when the astronaut misplaced his uniform?
_____ 5. Who was the first person in the universe?
_____ 6. Who wrote the book *Curing the Monotone Voice?*
_____ 7. What kind of long-distance calls do monks make when they speak to each other?
_____ 8. Who wrote the book *Magnificent Monogamy?*
_____ 9. How do you know that carrots are good for the eyes?
_____ 10. Who wrote the book *How To Be One of A Kind?*
_____ 11. Who wrote the book *Unison Singing?*
_____ 12. What kind of speech did the ugly duckling give when he grew up?

    a. "Holy smoke!"
    b. The man in the moon
    c. I. Will and Mary Yew
    d. A swan-ologue
    e. To a knight club
    f. Chris P. Chicken
    g. Parson-to-parson (person-to-person)
    h. Have you ever seen a rabbit wearing a monocle?
    i. U. Neek
    j. He lost his zip
    k. Al Toe Gether
    l. Dulles Dishwater

WORKING WITH
-MONO-, -UNI-
WORDS

Rootster has three new friends. One is a monarch, one is a monk and one is a monopolist. Help Rootster get his friends' traits straightened out. Write the correct code letter by each statement below.

a = the monarch
b = the monk
c = the monopolist

_____ 1. Gives lengthy monologues about his successful business empire
_____ 2. Has the unique privilege of creating national holidays
_____ 3. Wears a monocle and a military uniform
_____ 4. Stresses monogamy and performs unions
_____ 5. Wants to expand his business throughout the entire universe
_____ 6. Chants prayers in a monotone voice
_____ 7. Wears his country's monogram on a large ring
_____ 8. Wants to spread his message of faith over the entire universe
_____ 9. Wants to expand his power through the entire universe
_____ 10. Has a monogram of his religion embroidered on his robe
_____ 11. Travels all over the world selling his products
_____ 12. Has his company logo, a monogram, printed on every article of clothing he wears
_____ 13. Seldom leaves the monastery
_____ 14. Seldom leaves his capital city

Write **yes** beside the statements below that the monarch, the monk, and the monopolist would all agree with. Write **no** beside the statements that they would disagree about.

_____ 15. Being good at your work requires total commitment.
_____ 16. Business rules the world.
_____ 17. Loyalty to country counts most.
_____ 18. A leader's life must be an example for others to follow.
_____ 19. Only faith matters.

-BI-, -DU- two

biceps	*biped*
bicycle	*dialogue*
bifocal	*dissect*
bigamy	*duel*
bilingual	*duet*
binoculars	*duplex*
	duplicate

Unit Kickoff

Studying ancient Latin and Greek roots can help build a good vocabulary of modern words. Teach your students how to *dissect* a word. With the class, break the word *duplicate* into the parts, du-, -plic- and -ate. Then analyze the meaning of each part. In this case, du- indicates the quantity two; -plic- comes from the Latin plicare, to fold; and the suffix -ate means to make. Knowing the meanings of the parts of an unfamiliar word can help us unravel its definition.

Word Exploration Ideas

Secretly challenge three students to pantomime the sections of a *bicycle*. Have one student act as the rear wheel, one as the front wheel, and one as the handle bars. See if the class can guess the object that is being dramatized.

The history of *dueling* is a good topic for independent research. Challenge your students to find the answers to these questions: What does the dueling phrase "to give satisfaction" mean? When was dueling first outlawed in the United States? What weapons were most often used in duels? What famous Americans fought duels?

Invite student singers or musicians to perform a *duet* for the class!

Bilingual employees are becoming increasingly valuable in the business world. Ask your students to share their experiences with bilingual speakers. Have the students discuss which second languages might be the most useful at this time. Encourage them to give reasons for their choices.

Wake up your students' sluggish brain cells! Surprise your language class with some calisthenics designed to build *biceps*. Ask athletically-inclined students to plan and direct a mini-workout. Encourage them to find out and explain how the arm muscles function.

READING FOR MEANING
-BI-, -DU-
two

CRR-INCH!

CRR-UNCH!

CR-INCH!

CR-UNCH!

Rootster finishes his breakfast of cold cereal and begins the day's *dialogue* with his passengers.

"In a few minutes," he announces, "we will land in the region where breakfast cereals were first created. Here is how it may have happened. Back in the 1890s, Dr. Crispus Kruncher left his *duplex* early one morning to ride his *bicycle* into the countryside. Through his *binoculars,* he saw fields of healthy cattle eating grain. Could *bipeds* benefit from a similar diet, he wondered?

"Back home, he *dissected,* analyzed, and mixed different types of grain, trying to *duplicate* the healthful mixture that the cows thrived on. Dr. Kruncher believed that his new food would build strong *biceps*, eliminate the need for *bifocals*, prevent *bigamy*, and even aid in folks' attempts to become *bilingual*!

"Dr. Kruncher's efforts resulted in a hard cereal that was difficult to eat. Eventually he flattened the chunks into flakes. Crunchy cereal crackling in cold milk became the *duet* that got Americans going in the mornings. Other companies followed his lead and came out with their own flavors of cereal."

Everyone in our group chuckles as the plane lands. Once again, Rootster is revising history for our entertainment.

ROOTING FOR MEANING
-BI-, -DU-

Write definitions for the boldfaced words. Refer to a dictionary. Include a root meaning (two) in each definition.

Example: biped—a creature with two feet.

ROOTSTER'S **-BI-, -DU-** RIDDLES

Oops! Rootster's pen is running out of ink! Finish these riddles
for him by filling in the missing vocabulary words.

biceps
bicycle
bifocals
bigamist
bi-knock-knock-ulars
bilingual
biped
dialogue
dissect
duel
duets
"dew"-plex (duplex)
dupli-gator

1. Which fish like to sing _____? Tuna fish.

2. What did one banana say to the other banana when the cook
   tried to _____them? "Let's split!"

3. What kind of _____ live in the sea? Mussels.

4. Why can't a _____ stand up by itself?
   Because it's two-tired.

5. Where do raindrops live? In a _____.

6. Why did the _____ stand on one leg? Because if he lifted it, he would fall down.

7. A woman married two men, both named Ed.Why did she become a _____?
   Because two Eds are better than one.

8. Who wrote, "Oh Say Can You See?" Someone in need of new _____.

9. How do you know that whales enjoy _____? Because they are always spouting
   off with one another.

10. What do mermaids use in a _____? Swordfish.

11. What's the hardest thing about becoming _____? Getting a second tongue!

12. What do you call the mother of twin reptiles? _____.

13. What optical device helps you spot a bad joke a mile away? _____.

WORKING WITH
-BI-, -DU-
WORDS

Rootster reports the latest news from Toyland! Match each nursery rhyme headline with a detail from the list at the bottom of the page.

_____	1. London Bridge Is Falling Down
_____	2. St. Ives Man Has Seven Wives
_____	3. Blackbirds Found in King's Pie
_____	4. Big Ship Spotted, A-Sailing on the Sea
_____	5. Tweedledee and Tweedledum Agree At Last
_____	6. Bo-Peep Has Lost Her Sheep
_____	7. Piper's Son Tom Steals Pig . . .
_____	8. King of Spain's Daughter Visits Nut Tree
_____	9. Ring Around The Rosie
_____	10. Wee Willie Winkie Seen in Nightgown
_____	11. Gregory Griggs Has 27 Different Wigs
_____	12. Crooked Man and Crooked Cat

a. Girl Uses Bifocals to Find Flock

b. No Bicycles Allowed Across

c. None of Them are Duplicates

d. Voted Best New Game for Young Bipeds

e. Bilingual Discussions Produce Golden Apples & Silver Pears

f. A Duel Settles Their Differences

g. Charged With Bigamy

h. Claims He Was Lifting Heavy Object to Exercise Biceps

i. Now Performing Unique Duets Nightly at Rootster's Rock-a-Dome

j. Boy With Binoculars Beats Communications Satellite

k. Checks Duplexes Nightly

l. Royal Cook Dissects It

NUMBER ROOTS

centenarian
century
decade
decimate
Pentagon

quadrilateral
quart
quarter
quintuplet
quintessence

triangle
triathlon
tricycle
trio

Unit Kickoff

Introduce the unit number words by asking the vocabulary-related questions below. Have students jot down their answers. Allow them to change their answers once they know the correct meaning of each word.

    1. Are you a centenarian?
    2. Would you like to be a quintuplet?
    3. Should your teacher decimate you?
    4. Are you part of any trio?

Additional words derived from number roots are centigrade, centennial, centime, centimeter, centipede, centurion, Decalogue, decapod, decathlon, decibel, December, pentadactyl, pentameter, pentarchy, pentathlon, pentatonic, Pentecost, quadrant, quadrennial, quadrille, quadrivium, quarto, quatrefoil, Triassic, tribune, tricolor, trigonometry, trinity, triumvirate, trivia, and troika.

Word Exploration Ideas

The **Pentagon** houses the departments of the Army, Navy, and Air Force. It covers 29 acres and has about 3,706,000 square feet of office space and approximately 100,000 miles of telephone cable. Have students research to learn about activities that take place at the Pentagon.

Relate vocabulary to the Olympics! Direct your sports-minded students to determine the different contests that make up a **decathlon**, a **pentathlon** and a **heptathlon**. The **triathlon** is not an Olympic event. It usually includes running, biking and swimming.

READING FOR MEANING
NUMBER ROOTS

Rootster, are we in Canada?

"Yes!" Rootster smiles. "Ontario to be exact. We are heading for the town of Callandar, home of the Dionne *quintuplets*, the first quintuplets known to have reached adulthood. When news of the babies' birth was released over six *decades* ago, the continent went wild. Their birth was a major news event of the twentieth *century*.

"The five little Dionnes were the *quintessential* baby girls. People sent presents, probably items such as *tricycles*, *quarts* of milk, and *quarters* for the babies' piggy banks. It is rumored that a kind *centenarian* from Kansas sent a *trio* of canaries, and another donor may have made educational toys—wooden blocks carefully cut into *triangles* and *quadrilaterals*. Some people say that when World War II began, an official at the *Pentagon* invited the Dionne family to visit the American soldiers stationed in Washington, D.C.

"For the girls, growing up in the public eye must have been like an endless *triathlon,* with trials that could have *decimated* their childhood. But the girls endured the curiosity and the questions. They grew up to become normal adults, leading quiet, private lives."

ROOTING FOR MEANING
NUMBER ROOTS

Write definitions for the boldfaced words. Refer to a dictionary. Include the appropriate number root meaning in each definition.

Example: decade - a time period of ten years

ROOTSTER'S **NUMBER ROOT** RIDDLES

The answers to some more great vocabulary riddles are listed below.
Write down the number of the matching question beside each one.

_____ A. A tot rod

_____ B. One trains to run, the other runs the train.

_____ C. "Cheer up! It's hip to be square!"

_____ D. The Bentagon

_____ E. A scent-ury

_____ F. Quintuplets on roller skates

_____ G. Because dimes have changed

_____ H. "Order in the quart!"

_____ I. A box of quackers

_____ J. It has four quarters.

_____ K. The marryin' centenarian

_____ L. A try-angle

1. What did the rectangle say to the equal-sided quadrilateral?
2. What do you call a 100-year old man looking for a new wife?
3. What do you get if you put a trio of ducks in a carton?
4. What did people call the five-sided building in Washington, D.C., after a tank crashed into it?
5. What do you call a fast tricycle?
6. What is the difference between a triathlete and a locomotive engineer?
7. Why isn't ten cents worth what it was a decade ago?
8. What moves along on 40 wheels?
9. What did the judge say to calm the rowdy milk bottles?
10. Which geometric shape never gives up?
11. Why is the moon like a dollar?
12. How long does a skunk's smell last?

WORKING WITH
NUMBER ROOTS

Sharpen your pencil and your wits! Solve Rootster's brain teasers.

1. Quintuple the number of events in a triathlon. How many events in all?_____

2. A terrible illness has decimated the population of a region. According to the root meaning of the word, what percentage of the population has been affected? _____

3. In how many decades will a 70-year old be a centenarian? _____

4. A mother gives birth to a set of triplets and later to quintuplets.

   How many babies in all?_____

5. According to its name (not the actual calendar), which is the tenth month? _____

6. If you have a triangle, a pentagon, and a quadrilateral, how many sides do you have?

   _____

7. How long would you need to become bilingual, a century or a decade?

   Include the meaning of the vocabulary words in your answer._____

   _____

8. What is one quarter of a gallon? _____

9. You own a unicycle, a tricycle, and a bicycle. How many wheels in all? _____

10. The United States of America became independent in 1776. When will the nation celebrate its quadricentennial? _____

11. You attend a concert at which a trio performs first. The other act is a duet. How many performers in all? _____

12. Create your own quintathlon. List the events. _____

-SYM-, -SYN- together, same

photosynthesis	*symphony*	*syndicate*
symbiosis	*symposium*	*synthetic*
symbol	*symptom*	
symmetric	*synagogue*	
sympathy	*synchronize*	

Unit Kick-off

Use a symmetrical art project to get students thinking of the root definition *same.* Pass out 8 ½" x 11" sheets of construction paper. Have each student fold his or her paper in half lengthwise, keeping the fold at the bottom. Next, have the students write their signatures in large letters, pressing down very hard with a ballpoint pen or pencil. (Tell students to line up their letters as close to the fold on their paper as possible.) When they unfold their paper, they will see the signature on the other side of the fold line. Have the students use colorful markers and crayons to turn their names into *symmetrical* designs.

Word Exploration Ideas

Here's a challenge for your budding actors. Gather several students and give them a few minutes to read up on the process of *photosynthesis.* Then have them dramatize the process for the class. See if the rest of the students can identify what the group is acting out.

How many different types of *symbols* can students list? Some they might mention are map legends, meanings associated with different colors, hobo symbols, American Indian trail signs, operational signs in mathematics, abbreviations on the periodic table, and ranchers' branding symbols. The list is endless. Assign each student the task of compiling a handbook for one common category of symbols.

Since ancient times, synagogues have served as places of worship, uniting people in prayer and study. If possible, tour a local *synagogue* with your class, or invite a rabbi to describe the synagogue's role in Jewish life.

Everyone knows the *symptoms* of the dreaded ailments—spring fever, falling in love, and senior-itis. For fun, have the students write medical-sounding descriptions of these sometimes very real conditions.

The challenge of conducting a *symphony* orchestra is to make many instruments play together as one unit. Send students to the library to research the types of instruments used in a symphony.

READING FOR MEANING
-SYM-, -SYN-
together, same

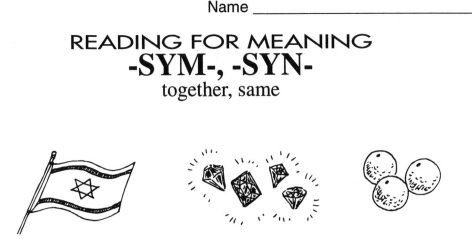

His **symptoms** are those of a crazy man, but in reality, Rootster is just extremely excited. We land in Israel, and our pilot tells the story of the young nation with great **sympathy**.

"Following World War II, thousands of Jews had no home. Delegates to the United Nations held a **symposium** on the problem. After much discussion, they came up with a plan to **synthesize** a Jewish homeland from sections of Palestine. **Synagogues** around the world **synchronized** their celebrations, and on May 14, 1948, the new nation of Israel became official.

"Almost overnight, it seemed, the land bloomed. The desert sun made it possible for **photosynthesis** to take place. A bumper crop of citrus fruit was produced. Skilled diamond-cutters from Europe brought their craft with them, teaching others to make tiny **symmetrical** cuts on natural and **synthetic** stones. Business **syndicates** organized to market Israeli products abroad. Musicians quickly assembled a **symphony** orchestra so the new nation would have music.

"Israel continues to thrive. But the region has also known great suffering as Jews and Arabs have faced the difficult challenge of living in **symbiosis**. Today Israel is a **symbol** for perseverance and commitment."

ROOTING FOR MEANING
-SYM-, -SYN-

Write definitions for the boldfaced words. Refer to a dictionary. Include a root meaning (together or same) in each definition.
Example: synchronize—to set at the same time

ROOTSTER'S -SYM-, -SYN- RIDDLES

Unscramble these riddles for some side-splitting vocabulary fun! Write the letter of the correct answer beside each question.

_____ 1. How are synchronized watches like twins?
_____ 2. What did the boy symphony member say to the girl symphony member?
_____ 3. According to scientists, when does most photosynthesis occur?
_____ 4. What do you call a doctor that feels as sick as you do?
_____ 5. What do you call it when you fall in love with a female specter?
_____ 6. Why did Elvis sing the blues about his synthetic shoes?
_____ 7. What do you call an absence of symptoms in the nasal passages?
_____ 8. What did the group of businessmen name their new kitten?
_____ 9. What do you call a symposium of scoundrels, sneaks, and rascals?
_____10. Why did the sign yawn when new symbols were pasted on it?
_____11. What did the animal trainer call his twin dog act?
_____12. What's another name for false teeth?
_____13. Who croaked in the house of worship?

  a. A cheating meeting
  b. Syndi-cat
  c. He found out they were man-made suede.
  d. "We make beautiful music together!"
  e. It's not easy to tell which watch is which.
  f. On Sundays
  g. Because it was a bill bored
  h. A sympathetic medic
  i. Ghostess symbiosis
  j. Synthe-cisors
  k. The synagogue frog
  l. Minus sinus
  m. A symmetric pet trick

WORKING WITH
-SYM-, -SYN-
WORDS

photosynthesis	symphony	synchronize
symbiosis	symposium	syndicate
symbol	symptoms	synthesize
symmetrical	synagogue	synthetic
sympathy		

Right these wrongs. Each sentence here uses a vocabulary word in an incorrect way. Cross out the incorrect word and right the correct word on the line.

1. Despite their age difference there was a touching photosynthesis between the old man and his little grandson. _____

2. We must syndicate our watches so we will leave at the same time. _____

3. What are the symbols of scarlet fever? _____

4. After my grandfather died, I marveled that so many people sent me kind notes of symbiosis. _____

5. Charles Goodyear experimented for years before he found a successful formula for symmetric rubber. _____

6. When the symposium orchestra began to play, the stirring notes of the overture filled the auditorium. _____

7. Green plants produce their own food through the process of symmetry. _____

8. At sundown on Friday, the Jewish Sabbath begins, and worshippers fill the symphony. _____

9. An outstretched hand is the universal sympathy of friendship. _____

10. The mark of a good student is the ability to synchronize new ideas from bits and pieces of existing data. _____

11. Our hostess placed the chairs in two symptomatic groupings. _____

12. The owner of our local newspaper joined with other small town papers to form a national synagogue. _____

13. At the stylists' synthetic, the hair dresser learned the latest techniques in cutting and curling. _____

Answer Key

Page 3
1. e 5. h 9. b
2. c 6. a 10. g
3. d 7. l 11. k
4. i 8. j 12. f

Page 4
1. c 5. h 9. l
2. i 6. j 10. k
3. f 7. e 11. g
4. d 8. a 12. b

Page 7
1. c 5. b 9. i
2. d 6. j 10. k
3. a 7. g 11. f
4. e 8. l 12. h
        13. m

Page 8
Sentences will vary.

Page 11
1. c 5. j 9. l
2. f 6. h 10. k
3. i 7. b 11. d
4. a 8. e 12. g

Page 12
1. Pig #2 4. Pig #9 7. Pig #1
2. Pig #5 5. Pig #10 8. Pig #4
3. Pig #7 6. Pig #3 9. Pig #6
        10. Pig #8

Page 15
1. f 5. c 9. k
2. g 6. j 10. a
3. e 7. b 11. i
4. h 8. d

Page 16
A Porter's Rules of Deportment
1. portcullis 6. portals
2. portfolio 7. import
3. portico 8. port
4. portage, portage, portage 9. transportation
5. portable 10. reporters

Page 19
1. e 5. i 9. b
2. g 6. c 10. f
3. a 7. d 11. h
4. j 8. l 12. k
        13. m

Page 20
1. gentleman, gender 6. generation
2. ingenious, indigenous 7. eugenics, genealogy
3. degeneration 8. regeneration
4. progeny 9. generic
5. genuine, gendarme

Page 23
A. 6 F. 12 K. 14
B. 2 G. 7 L. 3
C. 13 H. 1 M. 11
D. 10 I. 9 N. 5
E. 4 J. 8

Page 24
1. h 6. i 11. j
2. d 7. m 12. n
3. k 8. e 13. g
4. f 9. o 14. l
5. a 10. b 15. c

Page 27
1. e 5. a 9. c
2. f 6. i 10. d
3. g 7. b 11. k
4. h 8. j

Page 28
1. d 5. k 9. f
2. g (or c) 6. e 10. c (or g)
3. j 7. h 11. i
4. a 8. b

Page 31
1. Famous 8. Nom de plume
2. Unknown 9. Bubble
3. Surname 10. Denominator
4. Worm 11. Synonym
5. Nomer 12. Too
6. Nominate 13. Antonym
7. Pseudonym

Page 32
1. High-Fat 6. Cuddle
2. Ah-Choo 7. Whisper
3. Shy Pearl 8. High Order of Evil Enchanted Beings
4. May I Sing 9. Yawn
5. Yawn 10. Low-Fat

Page 35
1. d 5. i 9. l
2. g 6. f 10. b
3. a 7. c 11. e
4. h 8. j 12. m
        13. k

Page 36
1. smitten 7. Submit
2. missionary 8. intermittent
3. commissaries 9. missile
4. admit 10. commitment
5. permits 11. remittance
6. missives 12. messages
        13. committee

Page 39
A. 5 F. 3 K. 11
B. 6 G. 2 L. 8
C. 13 H. 7 M. 14
D. 4 I. 15 N. 1
E. 10 J. 9 O. 12

Page 40
Sentences will vary.

Page 43
1. c 5. a 9. f
2. d 6. h 10. j
3. b 7. k 11. g
4. e 8. l 12. i

Page 44
1. d 5. c 9. b
2. h 6. a 10. l
3. j 7. e 11. m
4. k 8. f 12. g
        13. i

Page 47
1. h 5. m 9. a
2. d 6. b 10. i
3. f 7. l 11. e
4. k 8. j 12. g
        13. c

Page 48
1. injection 7. object
2. jetty 8. jetsam
3. dejection 9. projectile
4. trajectory 10. conjectured
5. subject 11. interjections
6. jettisoned 12. jet
        13. rejection

Page 51
1. j 5. a 9. d
2. i 6. e 10. g
3. h 7. l 11. c
4. b 8. f 12. k

Page 52

1.	d	6.	k	11.	i
2.	g	7.	m	12.	f
3.	b	8.	n	13.	h
4.	j	9.	c	14.	l
5.	a	10.	e		

Page 55

A.	4	F.	1	K.	12
B.	8	G.	9	L.	2
C.	6	H.	14	M.	5
D.	10	I.	11	N.	3
E.	7	J.	13		

Page 56

1.	k	6.	m	11.	l
2.	i	7.	f	12.	e
3.	d	8.	j	13.	b
4.	a	9.	c	14.	g
5.	h	10.	n		

Page 59

1.	d	5.	l	9.	c
2.	g	6.	a	10.	m
3.	e	7.	j	11.	b
4.	f	8.	k	12.	h
				13.	i

A.	13	E.	1	I.	4
B.	12	F.	9	J.	7
C.	2	G.	10	K.	3
D.	5	H.	6	L.	8
				M.	11

Page 60

1.	manicuring	5.	manage	9.	manure
2.	maneuvers	6.	manacles	10.	manifested
3.	Emancipate	7.	manner	11.	mandatory
4.	mandate	8.	manipulate	12.	manual
				13.	manufacture

Page 63

1.	f	5.	a	9.	m
2.	k	6.	d	10.	b
3.	c	7.	h	11.	i
4.	l	8.	g	12.	j
				13.	e

Page 64

1.	j	5.	e	9.	a
2.	l	6.	f	10.	c
3.	h	7.	d	11.	m
4.	i	8.	b	12.	k
				13.	g

Page 67

1.	f	6.	k	11.	m
2.	i	7.	d	12.	h
3.	j	8.	a	13.	n
4.	g	9.	e	14.	c
5.	b	10.	l		

Page 68
Sentences will vary.

Page 71

A.	5	E.	4	I.	12
B.	8	F.	1	J.	6
C.	3	G.	10	K.	9
D.	7	H.	11	L.	2

Page 72
Sentences will vary.

Page 75

1.	inspect	8.	speculate
2.	species	9.	spectators
3.	circumspect	10.	spectacle
4.	expects	11.	inconspicuous
5.	spectrum	12.	introspective
6.	retrospective	13.	specter, specter
7.	suspicious		

Page 76

1.	introspection	7.	conspicuous
2.	spectrum	8.	suspicious
3.	species	9.	inspected
4.	circumspect	10.	spectacles
5.	speculated	11.	expect
6.	spectator	12.	specter
		13.	retrospect

Page 79

1.	f	5.	b	9.	h
2.	e	6.	l	10.	i
3.	a	7.	g	11.	k
4.	j	8.	c	12.	d

Page 80

1.	c	8.	b	15.	yes
2.	a	9.	a	16.	no
3.	a	10.	b	17.	no
4.	b	11.	c	18.	yes
5.	c	12.	c	19.	no
6.	b	13.	b		
7.	a	14.	a		

Page 83

1.	duets	7.	bigamist
2.	dissect	8.	bifocals
3.	biceps	9.	dialogue
4.	bicycle	10.	duel
5.	dew-plex	11.	bilingual
6.	biped	12.	dupli-gator
		13.	bi-knock-knock-ulars

Page 84

1.	b	5.	f	9.	d
2.	g	6.	a	10.	k
3.	l	7.	h	11.	c
4.	j	8.	e	12.	i

Page 87

A.	5	E.	12	I.	3
B.	6	F.	8	J.	11
C.	1	G.	7	K.	2
D.	4	H.	9	L.	10

Page 88

1.	15	8.	a quart
2.	10%	9.	6
3.	3	10.	2176
4.	8	11.	5
5.	December	12.	Answers will vary.
6.	12		
7.	a decade		

Page 91

1.	e	5.	i	9.	a
2.	d	6.	c	10.	g
3.	f	7.	l	11.	m
4.	h	8.	b	12.	j
				13.	k

Page 92

1.	symbiosis	8.	synagogue
2.	synchronize	9.	symbol
3.	symptoms	10.	synthesize
4.	sympathy	11.	symmetrical
5.	synthetic	12.	syndicate
6.	symphony	13.	symposium
7.	photosynthesis		